INTERMEDIATE *and* ADVANCED

PUNCH NEEDLE
RUG HOOKING

INTERMEDIATE and ADVANCED

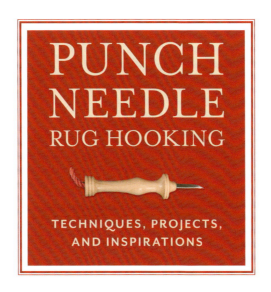

PUNCH NEEDLE RUG HOOKING

TECHNIQUES, PROJECTS, AND INSPIRATIONS

AMY OXFORD

with LOUISE KULP

PHOTOGRAPHY BY DAVID STANKOSKI

Featuring the Work of 26 Oxford Certified Instructors

SCHIFFER CRAFT

4880 Lower Valley Road • Atglen, PA 19310

OTHER SCHIFFER CRAFT BOOKS BY AMY OXFORD:

Punch Needle Rug Hooking: Your Complete Resource to Learn & Love the Craft, ISBN 978-0-7643-6015-2
Hooked Rugs Today, photog. by Cynthia McAdoo, ISBN 978-0-7643-2152-8
Hooked Rugs Today: Strong Women, Flowers, Animals, Children, Christmas, Miniatures, and More, photog. by Cynthia McAdoo, ISBN 978-0-7643-2578-6
Hooked Rugs Today: Holidays, Geometrics, People, Animals, Landscapes, Accessories, and More, photog. by Cynthia McAdoo, ISBN 978-0-7643-2636-3
Hooked Rugs Today IV: Expect the Unexpected, ISBN 978-0-7643-3283-8

OTHER SCHIFFER CRAFT BOOKS ON RELATED SUBJECTS:

Welcome to Weaving: The Modern Guide, Lindsey Campbell, ISBN 978-0-7643-5631-5
Rug Hooking with Wool Strips: 20 Contemporary Projects for the Modern Rug Hooker, Katie Kriner, ISBN 978-0-7643-6209-5
Punch Needle Extravaganza! 27 Projects to Create, Laetitia Dalbies, ISBN 978-0-7643-6258-3

Copyright © 2024 by Amy Oxford

Library of Congress Control Number: 2023941113

"The Oxford Punch Needle®" and logo are registered trademarks owned by The Oxford Company, LLC.

All of the rugs and other punch needle pieces shown in this book are punched on 100% cotton monk's cloth backing unless otherwise noted. No monks were harmed in the making of this book.

Portions of chapter 6 originally appeared in *Rug Hooking* magazine vol. XXXII, September/October 2020. Republished with permission from *Rug Hooking* magazine.

Photographs on pages 99, 159 bottom, 204, 210, 211, 212 top & center, 232 are by Anne-Marie Littenberg.

All rights reserved. No part of this work may be reproduced or used in any form or by any means—graphic, electronic, or mechanical, including photocopying or information storage and retrieval systems—without written permission from the publisher.

The scanning, uploading, and distribution of this book or any part thereof via the Internet or any other means without the permission of the publisher is illegal and punishable by law. Please purchase only authorized editions and do not participate in or encourage the electronic piracy of copyrighted materials.

"Schiffer Craft" and the crane logo are registered trademarks of Schiffer Publishing, Ltd.

Designed by Ashley Millhouse
Cover design by Ashley Millhouse
Cover and frontispiece images: Coral Mat. Designed by Cotey Gallagher. Color planned and punched by Amy Oxford.
Type set in Mrs Eaves/Mr Eaves San

ISBN: 978-0-7643-6757-1
Printed in China

Published by Schiffer Craft
An imprint of Schiffer Publishing, Ltd.
4880 Lower Valley Road
Atglen, PA 19310
Phone: (610) 593-1777; Fax: (610) 593-2002
Email: Info@schifferbooks.com
Web: www.schifferbooks.com

For our complete selection of fine books on this and related subjects, please visit our website at www.schifferbooks.com. You may also write for a free catalog.

Schiffer Publishing's titles are available at special discounts for bulk purchases for sales promotions or premiums. Special editions, including personalized covers, corporate imprints, and excerpts, can be created in large quantities for special needs. For more information, contact the publisher.

We are always looking for people to write books on new and related subjects. If you have an idea for a book, please contact us at proposals@schifferbooks.com.

To my mother
Jane Esbenshade Breneman Kulp
—L.K.

To my daughter
Alaina Skye Dickason Roberts
—A.O.

A punch needle lover needs tools!

The Oxford Rug Hooking School in Cornwall, Vermont

Amy and Toby at work

Contents

Acknowledgments 9

Introduction 12
1. Novelty Yarns and Yarn Combinations 15
2. Using Different Punch Needle Sizes 39
3. Sculpting 71
4. Shading 101
5. Punching with Fabric Strips 133
6. Two-Color Beading Stitch 163
7. Shading with Yarn: A Painter's Approach 181
8. Telling Stories with Your Punch Needle 197
9. The Coral Project 215
10. Pieces to Learn From: Oxford Teacher Certification Rugs 223

Index 235
About the Authors 238

Louise sketching a new rug design

Amy with freshly dyed Violet Jane Rug Yarn

Winter view from The Oxford Rug Hooking School

Acknowledgments

Louise Kulp

I acknowledge Amy Oxford with professional gratitude too great to measure. I met Amy in 2006, and since that time she has been—in more or less chronological order—my teacher, mentor, and colleague. She has also always been my friend. I've lost track of the number of times I've been able to say, "If it wasn't for Amy, I wouldn't have _____" (fill in the blank with an amazing opportunity). The amazing opportunity to collaborate on this book is the latest example. But I am just one of the many fiber artists who has benefited from Amy's generosity. Time and again I have observed her offering up opportunities to others, and she always does so selflessly and with joy.

Amy and I were fortunate to have Margaret Mitchell proofread our book. There was no one better for the task. Margaret is also my dear friend and confidante, and I love her for it. My traditional rug-hooking teacher, Peggy Hannum, deserves special thanks for introducing me to fine shading and instilling in me a love of knobby scrolls and eight-value rose petals. To the staff at the Oxford Company—Hannah Harding, Christy Lombardo, Heidi Whipple, Dave Stankoski, and Cotey Gallagher—thank you for making my work look so good! Dave photographed my work with great care and expertise, and Cotey "computerized" my hand-drawn diagrams in a way that makes them still look hand-drawn. Thanks also to our editor, Sandra Korinchak and her team at Schiffer Publishing, for their guidance, care, and patience.

Personally I have been blessed with a solid family and a diverse group of friends. Among those dear to me, I want to especially thank my late mom, who was proud of me and my accomplishments, no matter how small. How I wish she could hold this book in her hands, and we could page through it together. I thank my beloved niece and life coach, Lynn, for telling me in no uncertain terms, "You're doing the book," and my sister and other life coach, Sally (apparently I need two . . .). I wish to thank the four Little Boys in my life. My grandnephews are all still too young to know what they mean to me, but someday I'll be able to tell them how they helped propel me forward.

Finally, I will forever be grateful to my friend Tedd for taking my work as seriously as I did, and to my far-flung rug friends for their collective inspiration, a gift they give me that fortunately is not bound by distance.

Amy Oxford

My sincerest thanks to my coauthor, Louise Kulp. I never would have attempted this book without her. Though Louise started as my student, I knew from the first day in class when she pulled out her sketch book that I would learn just as much from her. I learned a great deal from Louise while working together on this book, including punch needle techniques I never thought of and now can't do without. Equally important, I learned what true dedication, timeliness, and professionalism look like and that they are a gift you give to others. Her creativity, artistry, passion for the craft, projects, and narrative are the foundation of this book, and I am lucky to have her for a friend.

With love and enormous amounts of gratitude to my work family at the Oxford Company for their ongoing support and encouragement: Cotey Gallagher, who created all the illustrations, fine-tuned the diagrams, and didn't strangle me when I asked for multiple changes (I know it was tempting); Christy Lombardo, who skillfully dyed the yarn for some of the demo projects; Hannah Harding for her countless contributions and the impossible task of keeping *me* on task; Heidi Whipple for punching the demo version of the Flower Project, and for hiding the chocolate so I wouldn't eat it all; David Stankoski for patiently and skillfully taking all the photographs while simultaneously assembling and inspecting punch needles; Nancy Hall and Richard Phillip for all the care they put into each punch needle they assemble; and Sid Hansen, working quietly behind the scenes.

Wholehearted thanks to Oxford Certified Instructor Margaret Mitchell, my friend, for diligently proofreading this book and for her many years of dedication and service as a founding board member of The Oxford Punch Needle Instructors Guild.

Heartfelt thanks to all of the Oxford Certified Instructors and Advanced Oxford Certified Instructors who contributed work to this book. You've taken the advanced techniques and run with them! By challenging yourselves you encourage your students to do the same. Thank you for spreading your love of punch needle rug hooking and for keeping our craft alive! With special thanks and gratitude to Oxford Certified Instructor Margaret Mitchell for graciously writing her chapter, "Telling Stories with Your Punch Needle." It's an honor to feature her work and fascinating to learn about her design process. Thanks also to Oxford Certified

Instructor Colleen Faulkner for allowing me to highlight her rugs and share her perspective in her chapter, "Shading with Yarn: A Painter's Approach." Thanks to Oxford Certified Instructor Kevin LeMoine for telling us about punching with polar fleece and to Advanced Oxford Certified Instructor Judith Hotchkiss for sharing how she constructs her three-dimensional birds.

I am deeply grateful to my insightful editor, Sandra Korinchak at Schiffer Publishing, for her vision of the book, belief in me, and patience as months turned into years; to Pete Schiffer for asking for a new book; and to all of the Schiffer team.

Many thanks to my students and especially my longtime students from Fletcher Farm School for the Arts and Crafts. Without you, I might not have strived to learn these advanced techniques. Thank you for giving me a reason to explore new things to teach you! You have brought fresh insights and innovation to the techniques and a great deal of joy to my life. You have been my teachers too.

I doubt I would have ever become a rug hooker without the inspiration and guidance from my friends and mentors Cynthia and Preston McAdoo of McAdoo Rugs. This book is all your fault, and I mean that in a good way.

Because hooked rugs have no knots, I am often asked what keeps them from falling apart. The answer is that the loops are pressed so closely together they keep each other in place. Thank you to my loved ones for keeping me close so I don't unravel: Brewster Righter, Madora Cooke Soutter, Lindsay Boyer, Lucy Soutter, Morgan Cooke Soutter, Madora Comfort Soutter, Alaina Skye Dickason Roberts, Jonathan Roberts, Hattie Mae Roberts, Jonas Roberts, Iris Oxford, Andréa Borriello, R. Morgan Soutter, Melissa Schnirring, Suzanne Sawyer, Jay Leshinski, and Lee Greenewalt. My list feels incomplete without thanking my late mother and father, Julie Hattersley Righter and John D. Soutter.

Introduction

by Amy Oxford

I learned to make punch needle–style hooked rugs in 1982, when I worked for McAdoo Rugs, a cottage industry in North Bennington, Vermont. Known for their gorgeous and luxurious hooked rugs, they used the finest hand-dyed 100% wool rug yarn, monk's cloth, and the Craftsman's Punch Needle on setting 8 to create ½-inch loops. If you were lucky enough to have a McAdoo rug at your bedside . . . what a wonderful feeling to wake up and step onto such a lush, thick pile! Because the Craftsman is an adjustable tool, it can become "unadjusted" (Can't we all?), changing the loop height. To make sure all their rugs were uniform, McAdoo bent the setting on the tool so it would work only as a #8. For many years, that's all I used for work, but I couldn't resist the urge to play! Let's try all 10 settings! Let's put the different-sized loops side by side and clip them! I wonder if these chunky fibers would work? Or these silky ones? Let's try them all! It was a playground of unexplored approaches.

When I started teaching, I wanted something new to entice my students to come back time after time. It had to be something I had never seen done with a punch needle. A few of my ideas were wildly unpopular at the time but later caught on. For example, only one person signed up for a class to punch with fine yarn and a Craftsman's Punch Needle I adapted to make extra short loops. Now there is an Oxford Punch Needle in that size (fine #14), and classes are a hit!

I wanted a book that would teach some of these more specialized techniques and show examples of how to use them to enhance your work. I asked my friend and Advanced Oxford Certified Instructor Louise Kulp to join me. She designed the original projects (with the exception of Perfectly Paisley and the Coral Project, which were designed by Cotey Gallagher) and wrote excellent narrative instruction. My job was to punch the project step by step and photograph the process. I have chipped in with comments along the way, and I hope they will be helpful.

. A Note from Amy .

All of the Oxford Certified Instructors featured in this book are active teachers. At this time there are over 130 Oxford Certified Instructors in the US, Canada, the United Kingdom, Europe, the United Arab Emirates, and Japan. Many of them can be found on the Oxford Company website. Advanced Oxford Certified Instructors are trained to teach others to be Oxford Certified Instructors. There are now currently seven in the US, one in Germany, one in Ireland, and two in Canada. Certification courses are offered online, making the programs more accessible.

Having made all the projects, I can say that they are really enjoyable to work on, and I like the fact that they are small enough to create without the commitment, time, and expense of making larger rugs. There are so many fun new things you can do with your Oxford Punch Needles! This book will give you a taste of some of the many possibilities. I wouldn't be surprised if you invented some techniques of your own! Whether you choose to make the projects, just read along, or only look at the pictures (I am guilty of this with many how-to books), I hope that next time you work on something new, you will consider enriching your work with one or more of these ideas.

If a singer shares true emotion when singing a song, you can hear it and feel it. If you are truly excited about what you are making, others will see it, and the best part? You will feel it!

Punch on!

Amy xox

Amy Oxford
The Oxford Rug Hooking School

1

Novelty Yarns and Yarn Combinations

by Louise Kulp with contributions by Amy Oxford

THE SEASHELL PROJECT

Louise Kulp. *Seashell*. 8.75" × 8.75". Natural and synthetic fibers on cotton.

Pattern size: 8" × 8"

You will need:

- Monk's cloth size: 20" × 20" or size needed to fit your frame
- Oxford Gripper Strip Lap Frame: 10" × 10" or 14" × 14"
- #10 regular Oxford Punch Needle with screw eye in the bottom. (More on screw eyes later in this chapter.)
- Small, sharp embroidery scissors

Yarn needed:

- Assorted novelty yarns. Project as pictured uses wool, polyester metallic, cotton, rayon, acrylic, nylon, and polyamide.
- Yarn amounts needed: Novelty yarns for shell, background, and inner border, 45 yards. Rug yarn for outer border, 0.7 ounces.

For more about working with novelty yarns, please see Amy Oxford's companion book *Punch Needle Rug Hooking: Your Complete Resource to Learn & Love the Craft* (pages 93–97).

In a Nutshell

- Novelty yarns—those that are thick and thin, loopy, shiny, fuzzy, hairy, and sparkly—produce spectacular effects in punch needle rug hooking. Punchers can combine multiple novelties and thread them through the needle together or use one thick novelty by itself.

- Why is this an advanced technique? Novelty yarns behave in unexpected ways. They require more preparation, testing, time, and patience to work with, and often more punching experience.

- Novelty yarns typically are used to knit and crochet light-wear apparel and home décor accessories. They also can take the form of fancy threads that embroiderers use. Fortunately for us rug hookers, novelties open up a whole new world of creative potential.

- Many novelty yarns are not durable enough to use in rugs and other pieces that need to withstand wear. Save them for projects such as wall hangings, pillows, small purses, coasters, and tabletop decorations.

- Novelty yarns must be able to flow through the punch needle with enough ease to form consistent and continuous loops.

- Any size Oxford Punch Needle can be used.

- If you are using a regular point Oxford Punch Needle with multiple strands of fine yarn, it helps to have a screw eye on the bottom of the punch, but this is not essential.

- Novelties are a nice option when you don't have easy access to—or the budget for—hand-dyed rug yarn. Big-box craft stores carry a dizzying array.

- Caution: novelty yarns can melt or flatten drastically when steam-pressed.

CHOOSING NOVELTY YARNS AND YARN COMBINATIONS

(Note: to simplify terminology, this chapter uses "novelty yarn combinations," "novelties," and "combos" interchangeably. The word "yarn" is used for both yarn and thread.)

Before raiding your yarn stash, and those of your friends, relatives, colleagues, and neighbors (and then going shopping for more), it helps to be familiar with common properties of novelty yarns. Making appropriate choices for your new project will help ensure an enjoyable and successful punching experience and win admiration for your latest work of art. The yarns you choose will affect almost every aspect of your project, from what type of frame you should use, to punching technique, to steam pressing and end use. It is wise to plan ahead for smooth sailing from start to finish.

You can punch with almost any novelty yarn as long as it travels well through both the channel and the eye of the needle as you work, and makes the kind of loop you want. Some of the most beautiful and unusual effects achieved with this advanced technique are loops made from *yarn combinations*. By holding multiple yarns and threads together and punching them as one, you are creating a color and texture unique to your piece and to you as an artist.

VOCABULARY

Novelty yarns are made by using unorthodox spinning methods to create yarns that are not uniform along the length of a strand. They have intentional irregularities. In lay terms, novelty yarns are loopy, bumpy, slippery, hairy, sparkly, slubby, twisty, topsy, and turvy. Usually they are 100% synthetic or blends of synthetic and natural fibers.

Synthetic fibers are man-made from chemicals. Common examples are nylon, polyester, and acrylic. If that gorgeous skein of yarn you're dying to use has lost its label, assume it has some synthetic content, and treat it with care as you punch, press, and hem your project. If the skein is still wearing its label, the fiber content and care instructions will be on it.

Natural fibers come from animals and plants and include wool, silk, cotton, and linen.

Threads are fine cords or strings typically composed of multiple plies (or strands) spun together in a tight twist. They can be smooth or textured.

Novelty yarns can be thick and thin, loopy, shiny, fuzzy, hairy, and sparkly. They produce spectacular effects in punch needle rug hooking!

Likely you will be choosing yarns of wildly varying designs (just like you choose varying project designs). Examples of materials used in the Seashell Project include a skein of hand-dyed 100% wool rug yarn, a ball of cotton/acrylic/polyamide blend, and a spool of metallic thread. They range in weight from bulky to super fine. There is thick-and-thin yarn, velvety chenille, and a ball of straggly cotton intended for knitting scrubby bath mitts.

The choices can be overwhelming! When I gather novelties for a new project, I choose according to how I want to represent the elements in my design. For the Seashell Project I imagined a shell, just washed up on a sandy beach and glistening in the sun. The outer border represents the deep blue sea, and the inner border suggests foamy whitecaps. The whitecaps yarn combo includes a twisty cotton with short lengths of thread sticking out all over—perfect!

I made two values of sand simply by swapping out two darker strands in one combo for two lighter strands in the other, and leaving the third strand the same in both (*right*). We'll talk more about shading later in this chapter in "Creating multivalue combinations." Gold metallic embroidery thread and fine opalescent braid are the "strand-alongs" that gave me sparkle on the shell.

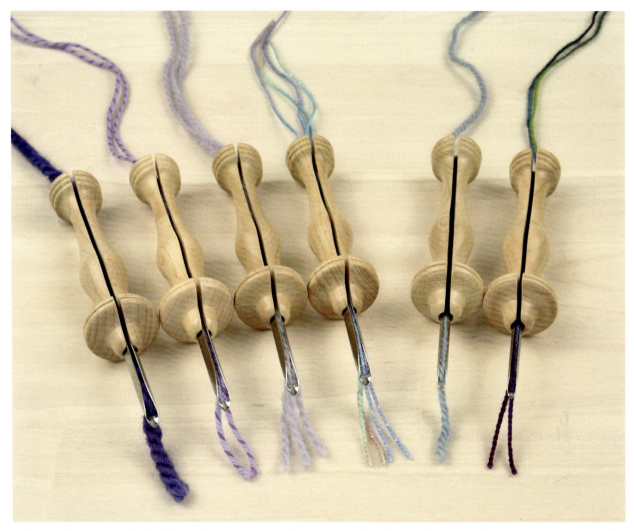

Left to right: Regular point Oxford Punch Needles threaded with rug yarn, double, triple, and quadrupled thinner yarn combinations, fine point Oxford Punch Needles threaded with worsted-weight yarn, and two strands of thinner yarn to match the thickness of the worsted.

I wanted three shades of blue green (one of my favorite colors, second only to pink!) in my project, but instead of swapping out a thread or two among combos like I did for the sand, I created three distinct shades all with different yarns, as you see in the photo at left. I call the colors aqua, turquoise, and teal (light to dark, respectively).

The Oxford Punch Needle comes with a stitch gauge to help you determine your stitch size and row spacing for rug-weight/bulky yarn (fiber from ⅛" up to ¼" thick). Newer Oxford stitch gauges now include this information for worsted-weight/fine yarn (fiber up to ⅛" thick). So you don't have to figure out a new stitch size and row spacing for every new yarn and yarn combination, try doubling, tripling, or even quadrupling thinner yarns to match the thickness of rug yarn. Similarly, you might need to use two strands of a thinner yarn to equal one strand of worsted-weight yarn.

NOVELTY YARNS AND YARN COMBINATIONS

Exploit the "noveltyness" of your yarns. You'll be surprised at the number of colors and textures you can get from just one ball of yarn. Look for those that change color or texture (or both) every few yards or so. These variations usually are long enough to punch an entire section of a project, while leaving several coordinating colors or textures intact to use elsewhere in your piece.

We mentioned earlier that the readily available yarns from big-box stores make the craft of punch needle rug hooking much more accessible. Knitting shops, although not as ubiquitous, also offer ready access to yarns. Most shops have a bargain or "oddball" section where that one last ball of luxury yarn ends up after its kinfolk have left the shop. Who is going to use that? Well, a rug hooker, that's who! Many oddballs contain expensive fibers such as cashmere and silk and can be had for a song.

If you're fortunate enough to have not only a knitting shop in your town but a needlework shop as well, by all means raid that too. This is where cross-stitchers and needlepointers go to buy specialty threads. The threads come on spools or are wound on small cards in several-yard lengths. They have fancy names like "Petite Treasure Braid," "Fuzzy Stuff," and "Silk 'N Colors," which is hand-dyed silk. Some threads come in plies that easily can be separated. "Silk 'N Colors," for example, has 12 plies, and you can use however many you want. Needlework threads can be pricey, but a little goes a long way in the special-effects department. Carried along with yarns, they add a certain je ne sais quoi to your project, *non*?

When choosing your yarns, plan ahead so you know how to handle your work in the finishing stage. Natural fibers can be steam-pressed just the way we're used to. Synthetics cannot, since heat and moisture will destroy the very properties that drew you to a yarn in the first place, such as texture, sparkle, or halo. Even blends such as cotton/polyester must be treated with extra care. I plan ahead to use 100% wool in the two (or more) outer rows of a novelty yarns project so I can steam-press at least the border.

NOVELTY YARNS AND YARN COMBINATIONS

MANAGING NOVELTY YARNS AND YARN COMBINATIONS

PREPARING YARN COMBINATIONS

Cut each yarn in your combination into a manageable three-yard length. I like to measure in "relaxed" yards; that is, letting my yarn lie naturally along a yardstick instead of stretching it out straight. Hold the ends together and thread them through your punch needle, then place the length beside you and arrange in a loose "puddle" (shown here). Doing so helps mitigate tangling and allows the yarns to feed freely through the punch needle.

If the yarns and threads in your combo are in center-pull balls, or wound on cones or spools, you can place everything in a large bowl, put it by your feet, and draw them out that way instead. This keeps the balls and cones from rolling all over the floor! Another option is to put your multiple balls of yarn for your combination in a large coffee can. Cut a hole in the center of the plastic lid and feed the yarn strands together through the hole.

You've chosen your yarns, and now it's time to see how they work. The two most important yarn characteristics to keep in mind are thickness (also called weight) and texture. Being mindful of these characteristics and learning how to manage them will result in the beautiful piece you have in your mind's eye.

Pro Tip: To make threading multiple yarns through the punch needle easier, twist the yarn ends together to make a tight little knob that can pass through the eye.

It can be difficult, at least early in your novelty yarns career, to know how many strands—and of what thicknesses—can go through the punch needle at the same time. It may help you to think of "equivalents." For a regular point needle, aim for a novelty combination equal to the thickness of rug-weight yarn. For a fine point needle, aim for the thickness of worsted-weight yarn. Here's an easy way to match thicknesses: interlocking twists of rug yarn and a combo of comparable thickness (*top*), and interlocking twists of worsted-weight yarn and a combo of comparable thickness (*bottom*).

It's not just the thickness of a yarn combo you have to consider, it's also the texture. It's perfectly fine—desirable even—to run all kinds of yarns through your punch needle, either alone or stranded together. The effects can be dazzling! But be aware that every novelty yarn has its own personality and will go through the needle its own way. An extremely textured yarn that you swear won't work may punch beautifully, while a smooth lustrous silk ends up a slippery disaster (known in some circles as yarn behaving badly). You won't know until you try.

Often, novelty yarn combinations result in loops that are irregular in shape and height and vary in color from loop to loop. Such variations are part of the charm of working with novelties. Be mindful, though, that you have to pay attention to things you normally don't when working with simple rug- and worsted-weight yarns. Punching with novelties can be unpredictable. You can embrace the serendipitous nature of your loops or you can control—to a certain extent—the look of them. Rise up to the challenge! We'll discuss how in the next section, "Punching with Novelty Yarns and Yarn Combinations."

I can get almost any novelty yarn to work for me *if* I have the patience to do so. What is *your* patience threshold? Decide for yourself if getting a desired effect outweighs the trouble it takes to achieve it. If I really, really want to use a bouclé for the center of a flower, I will, even if it means stopping midloop to desnag yarn from the tip of the needle *every single time* I plunge it down into the monk's cloth.

ADDITIONAL CONSIDERATIONS

Novelty yarns travel through punch needles at different rates. Some are speed demons (I'm looking at you, rayon) and others are slowpokes. Some snag on the needle tip every third stitch, and some punch as easily as the rug yarn we've come to know and love. Learn how each one's unique properties affect its behavior in the punch, and adjust your technique accordingly. For instance, as you approach the end of your yarn combo (assuming you're working with precut lengths), you may find that two of the original four strands are almost used up. If you keep going, the remainder of the loops will be skimpy and look different. To remedy this, simply cut the ends even again and finish the length.

DOODLE CLOTHS

If I had to choose only one thing as the absolute takeaway from this chapter, it is this: keep a doodle cloth. Commonly used by hand embroiderers, a doodle cloth is a piece of cloth kept handy to practice stitches on before you use them on your project. I heartily endorse them for rug-hooking projects too. It will save you time, frustration, heartbreak, and yarn.

Before embarking on the Seashell Project, I started a doodle cloth to test out my yarns. I put a spare piece of monk's cloth on a 10" square "Baby Ox" gripper strip frame and kept it close at hand, ready to test out novelty combinations. If you don't have an extra gripper strip frame, use a small carpet tack frame or a sturdy quilting hoop such as a Morgan No-Slip Hoop.

Louise's doodle cloth

Close-up of doodle cloth

Yarn combinations Louise tested on her doodle cloth

You will learn two things vital to the success of your project: (1) how different yarn combinations behave and (2) appropriate stitch size and row spacing. I never thought I'd say this, but *be prepared to disregard some rules you've learned about stitch size and row spacing.* Some of my combinations needed just four stitches per inch punched every other row in order to not "overpack" (close-up purple section at left). Others worked best punched four stitches per inch alternating with six stitches per inch and going in every row of monk's cloth (close-up pink section at right).

Remember that you are working to achieve a balance between technical and aesthetic considerations, and all of that can be worked out on a doodle cloth. In preparation for punching the Seashell Project, I tested 13 novelty yarn combinations. The ones that didn't punch well or give me the look I wanted got eliminated. By the end of my testing I had eight beautiful yarn combinations that I couldn't wait to use!

All of this experimenting before you even start your project may seem time consuming and a little cumbersome—and maybe it is—but soon you'll develop an instinct for what works and what doesn't.

NOVELTY YARNS AND YARN COMBINATIONS 27

PUNCHING WITH NOVELTY YARNS AND YARN COMBINATIONS

So far, we've talked about choosing novelty yarns, managing their unique properties, and keeping a doodle cloth to test them out. All of this knowledge will serve you well as you start to work on your design (*Finally!* I can hear you saying) and will help make your project fun to punch and a pleasure to display. The following points are included to supplement what you've already learned. Some will help get you out of trouble, and others will keep you from getting into it in the first place.

TOP TROUBLESHOOTING TIPS

- Check the front of your work frequently for loop irregularities. A row of novelty yarn loops can vary in height more so than a row made with simple yarn. Correct them as you go.

- Punch slower than usual—slowly enough to realize sooner rather than later that something is going awry.

- Be watchful that yarn is not snagging on the tip of the needle and preventing loops from forming. This is especially important when working with hairy or loopy yarns. If you have your heart set on using a yarn (as in "nothing else will do"), *and* you have the patience of a saint, you will stop and remove the snag by hand every time it happens.

- If you need to rip out, take care to pull each loop out completely. Don't leave behind any of the strands that make up the combination.

NOVELTY YARNS AND GRIPPER STRIP FRAMES

Use *extreme caution* when moving a novelty yarns project on a gripper strip frame, or do what I do and avoid it altogether. I design my novelty yarns projects to be only as large as my largest gripper strip frame, or I punch a design in segments and sew them together at the end. My theory—unscientific but logical—is that the "bundle" of strands we put together by hand to make a novelty yarn combination doesn't have the structural integrity of one that is commercially spun. I fear the loops would peel off the wire teeth all willy-nilly, with silk thread pulling out separately from slubby yarn, and so on. All I can picture in my mind is a wasteland of once-beautiful loops lying in a puddle of my own tears. Some of my colleagues have peeled fancy yarns right off gripper strips with nary a problem, but I'm still cautious. If you want to know for sure what will happen, try it out on your doodle cloth.

Pro Tip: Are your fine yarns slipping out of your punch needle slot? You're not alone! If you want the yarns in your combo to stay in the punch, travel through the needle at the same rate, and pretty much stay out of each other's way, you can use your nondominant hand to hold on to them with light tension about 6" away from where they enter the needle.

You can also insert a loose twist (*top*). I put the twist in by hand, but if I still had my spinning wheel I would use that to get a tight twist (*bottom*). Either of these techniques will make challenging yarns easier to punch with. You can use one or the other or both.

Using multiple strands of fine yarns in your regular point Oxford Punch Needle? A screw eye at the bottom of your punch can help fine yarns stay in the channel (right). The Oxford Company sells regular point Oxford Punch Needles with screw eyes by request. They can also add one to a punch you already own at no charge. (Note that screw eyes are not necessary for rug yarn or bulky-weight yarns. Fine point Oxford Punch Needles already have screw eyes.) **Caution:** It is VERY difficult to add a screw eye without cracking the handle or causing other problems. **Disclaimer:** Any damage to needles caused by alterations or manipulation of its original state will void the lifetime guarantee.

Despite your best efforts and the high level of patience you possess, the novelty yarn combinations you select for your design still may misbehave. Is your silk thread tangling with its thick-and-thin cotton neighbor (because darn if it doesn't take

NOVELTY YARNS AND YARN COMBINATIONS

two to tangle)? You may need to pause your punching from time to time to extricate one from the other. Is that slippery-as-an-eel rayon falling out of the needle even before it hits the monk's cloth? Punch it along with a textured yarn to give it some traction. You can think of the textured yarn as a "carrier" that helps the slippery yarn move through the punch, and the slippery yarn as a "strand-along" that hitches a ride with the carrier. Wool or other slightly fuzzy yarns often make great carriers.

Here's my one caveat for the troubleshooting tips above: you may not want to shoot *all* of your troubles! Not every puncher does. Strive for the effect that *you* want in *your* design. If you don't want all the loops the same height, that's fine! If you want the yarns to tangle, that's fine too, as long as they can make loops that way. Puncher's choice.

Does your hearty wool yarn obscure its fine gold companion? Take time when you're finished to make the gold bits more visible by gently pulling up on them with the points of your embroidery scissors.

SPECIAL EFFECTS

You might say that punching with novelty yarns already is one big special effect. True, but there are a few *extra*-special effects that are worth learning and adding to your repertoire of advanced techniques.

Tweeds

By chance I discovered (thank you, doodle cloth!) that putting a *tight* twist into a yarn combination before it enters the punch needle results in loops that have a tweedy appearance; the yarns get evenly distributed in a loop. The tighter the twist, the tweedier the loops. I used this technique for the sand in the Seashell Project because I wanted a consistently speckled look.

Stripes

Conversely, when I tried punching with no twist at all and just let the yarns go through the needle more or less in alignment, I got stripes. *Stripes!* (Shown top left and right.) I should caution, however, that if you're expecting yarns to travel through the needle "aligned," they should be mostly smooth or only slightly textured. This is an effective way to make directional punching apparent in a novelty yarns design. In the Seashell Project, I punched the turquoise flutes that radiate from the scallop shape this way to emphasize their strong vertical direction.

Creating multivalue combinations
Earlier I explained how I made two values of "sand" color for the background in the Seashell Project. That particular novelty combination has three different yarns in it, so I could have actually made four values of sand out of it by transitioning from light to dark this way (right): 3 light strands → 2 light and 1 dark → 1 light and 2 dark → 3 dark. Obviously, the more strands in a combination, the more values can be made.

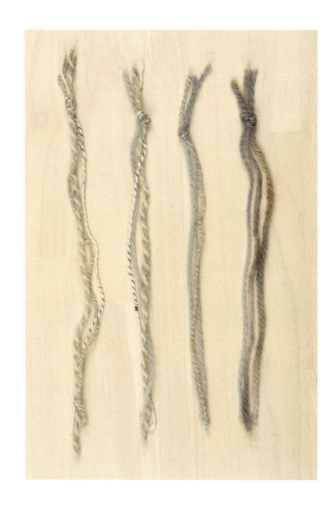

MAINTAINING SHAPES

I happen to be very "shape-centric" and don't always care for the way the unpredictability of novelty yarn loops can make shapes in my design look blobby. I remedy blobbiness by punching just inside the design lines. The Sharpie line should be barely visible. Doing this helps maintain contours by providing a little breathing space between design areas. It also is easier to poke loops into place to further define shapes.

SOMETIMES LESS IS MORE

Your novelty yarns project does not have to be made entirely of novelty yarns! Using special yarns sparingly and thoughtfully highlights their beauty and purpose. Another benefit of minimal novelty is having more possibilities for the end use of your piece. You can use novelty yarn in a rug or mat meant for the floor *if* the amount is modest. I used several novelty combinations in a floral garland I punched across the bottom of a rug. I placed the rug in a low-traffic area for extra caution.

FINISHING A NOVELTY YARNS PROJECT

It's so exciting to finish a work of art that you may be tempted to rush through the final steps of steam pressing and hemming. "I want to hang my beautiful new picture above my sofa, already!" Please be patient.

STEAM-PRESSING THE SEASHELL PROJECT

Aside from the actual punching, steam-pressing a novelty yarns project is the next most important part—truly a make-or-break moment and vital to the success of your piece. Sadly, many a novelty yarns project has been damaged (or even ruined) by errant steam pressing. If your yarns have any synthetic content at all, extra care must be taken.

I steam-press my wool rugs with a hot, dry iron—that is, with the steam setting off—and let a cold, wet towel generate the steam. We all know that 100% wool tolerates heat and steam well (as our collective steaming of thousands of wool rugs bears out), but the synthetic content of many (most?) novelty yarns does not.

Remember that synthetic yarn is man-made from chemicals. Melting, burning, matting, and crushing are the tragic results of heat on synthetics. You cannot unmelt yarn, so don't take the chance in the first place. Let experience and common sense guide you. That, and the yarn label if you still have it. Yarn labels show fiber content and care instructions. With novelties, you will often see a little symbol of an iron with an "X" through it. Don't steam that yarn! If you have any doubt at all how a yarn will press, regardless of its content, test-steam a patch on your doodle cloth.

I said earlier that I like to punch at least the two outside rows of a novelty yarns project with 100% wool so that I can steam-press the perimeter to help the piece lie flat. In the Seashell Project I steam-pressed only the dark-blue outer border made with wool rug yarn. If there are any other areas of steamable yarns in your design, use pins to cordon off the surrounding synthetics and *very carefully* press that which can be pressed.

Example of how to "cordon off" an area to protect novelty yarns and delicate fibers from being flattened or melted during steam pressing. Simply put pins around the delicate areas and iron around them. Think "police line—do not cross" or "fancy yarns—do not ruin!"

HEMMING

Take extra care in hemming your project. You don't want to catch the sewing needle on one strand and pull up part of a loop. Fine threads are especially susceptible.

Finally, if you are used to using a sweater depiller to defuzz your rug-yarn rugs, restrain yourself on pieces made with novelty yarns. The blades will cut delicate yarns (and I have personal experience to prove it!).

DOCUMENTING YOUR ARTWORK

I have praised the virtues of a doodle cloth *ad infinitum*. Are you dreaming about them yet?! I'll say just one more thing on the topic: a doodle cloth is a valuable record of the project you just finished. It documents the novelty yarn combinations that worked and the ones that didn't, and what you can steam and what you can't, and, if you dare to ask, it answers the question "Can I peel this yarn off gripper strip teeth without incident?" It will serve you well as a reference when planning your next design because you won't have to reinvent the wheel. You can make one for every project, or you can keep a "running" one on a larger frame to document multiple projects.

You also may want to keep a small bundle of each novelty yarn combination used in your project, because it can be difficult to see exactly what is in one just by looking at a loop. Make each bundle about 12" long and you'll have an easy-to-see record of your combinations.

A Note from Amy

WHAT I LEARNED FROM LOUISE ABOUT WORKING WITH NOVELTY YARNS

- I've never used a "doodle cloth" before. I've always done my testing right on my project in the area I wanted to fill in, creating unnecessary wear and tear on the backing. Now I'm a confirmed punch doodler!

- I learned the skill of emphasizing beautiful fibers that make higher loops. In yarn combinations, when one of the strands comes out taller than its fellow loops, Louise taught me to actually pull up on the taller loops to show them off (such as the thin gold threads in the shell). When you've got it—flaunt it!

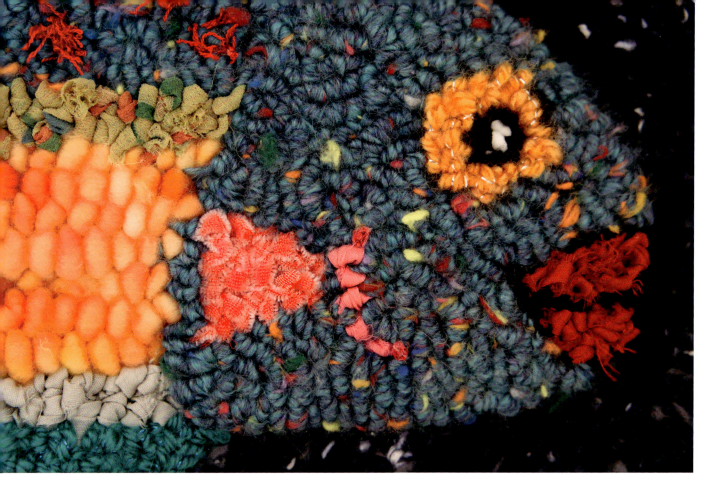

Funky Fish. Oxford Certified Instructor Yvonne Iten-Scott, Erin, Ontario, Canada. 15" × 8". Oxford regular #14 (background), Oxford fine #10 and Oxford regular #10 (fish). Tweed yarn (background); sari silk ribbon (tail, lower belly, gills, and lips); velvet strips (top fins); sparkle yarn (bottom fin and eye), chiffon strips (strips down the middle), speckled blue yarn combined with red eyelash yarn (head and top half of fish); chunky wool roving (bottom half of fish); white panty hose (eye).

"This was a fun piece to do. I always love using alternative fibers. The shine of the sari silk and sparkle yarn worked well to give the fish some life and I love the textures of the velvet and roving." Yvonne's Pro tip: "If you find the sari silk getting stuck in the needle, cut it down the middle."

Novelty Yarn Certification Sample. Advanced Oxford Certified Instructor Heidi Whipple, Cornwall, Vermont. 9.5" × 9.5". Punched with novelty fibers using all eight of the Oxford Punch Needle sizes: Oxford regular #8, #9, and #10 and Oxford fine #8, #9, #10, #13, and #14.

Novelty Yarn Certification Sample. Advanced Oxford Certified Instructor Kim Scanlan, St. Paul, Minnesota. 12" × 12". This piece uses a variety of novelty yarns in an Oxford regular #10.

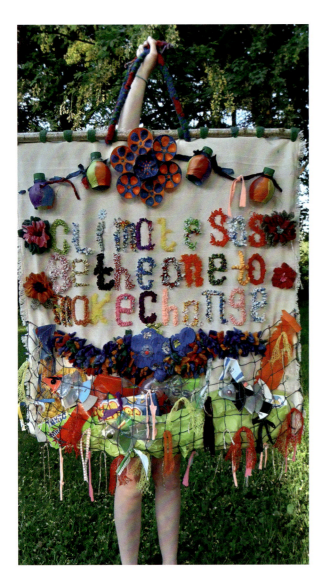 

Climate SOS - Be the One to Make Change. Oxford Certified Instructor Michelle O Driscoll, Cork, Munster, Ireland. 31" × 31". Oxford regular #9 and #13. Tissue paper; plastic sleeve from a milk carton (this was wonderful to punch with, and my favorite); cheap leather jewelry that you get on holidays (highlighting fast fashion); potato chip packets; netting from garlic and lemon bags; farm plastic; butter wrapper; nylon tights; popcorn packet; twine; paper hat from Christmas cracker; jersey T-shirt; Jiffy Cloth; string; and bread packet. Chinese lanterns made from painted plastic bottles.

"Having trained as an environmental scientist, I have always loved the outdoors and our environment. I spent a lot of my career working in the waste industry, so I found myself during lockdown rooting through my recycling bins and doing a lot of decluttering. I decided I would punch with whatever I could find in my recycling and garbage bin, and *Climate SOS – Be the One to Make Change* was born. As plastic in our seas is a big issue, I put a torn goal netting at the bottom and filled it with all the materials in my punched piece."

Branch. Advanced Oxford Certified Instructor Una Walker, La Grande, Oregon. 12" × 12". Oxford regular #8, #9, and #10 (branch, leaves, and border) and Oxford regular #13 (background). Wool yarns of different weights.

"Most of my work involves multiple strands and varying-height needles. I also use an Oxford regular #13 with a heavier yarn for great texture variation. I like the frame on this piece that incorporates the bead stitch and my method of using the stem stitch with two different colors in the needle."

2

Using Different Punch Needle Sizes

by Louise Kulp with contributions by Amy Oxford

Louise Kulp. *Puzzle of Love*. 8.75" × 8.75". Wool on cotton.

THE HEARTS SAMPLER

by Amy Oxford

ADAPTED FROM LOUISE KULP'S ORIGINAL *PUZZLE OF LOVE*

Hearts Sampler. 8.75" × 8.75". Wool on cotton. Punched by Amy Oxford.

USING DIFFERENT PUNCH NEEDLE SIZES

(If you would rather make a simpler loop-height sampler, please see the Simplified Hearts Sampler, starting on page 60.)

This sampler uses all eight Oxford Punch Needle sizes and the Craftsman's Punch Needle. If you do not have a Craftsman, you can use Oxford Punch Needles for the entire project. To do this, just alter the "map" slightly, replacing the areas that call for the Craftsman with Oxford Punch needle sizes of your choice.

Pattern size: 8" × 8"

You will need:

- Monk's cloth size: 20" × 20" or size needed to fit your frame
- 10" × 10" or 14" × 14" Oxford Gripper Strip Lap Frame
- Oxford Punch Needles #8, #9, and #10 regular point
- Oxford Punch Needles #8, #9, #10, #13, and #14 fine point
- Craftsman's Punch Needle
- A stitch gauge
- Small, sharp embroidery scissors

Yarn needed:

- 100% wool worsted-weight yarn for all of sampler. (Use a single strand of the worsted-weight yarn for all the fine point Oxford Punch Needles and two strands for all the regular point Oxford Punch Needles and the Craftsman's Punch Needle.)
- Approximately 5 ounces total in your choice of colors and values. Amy used four colors: pink, olive, dusty blue, and ocher. Each color has a light, a medium, and a dark value.
- The Hearts Sampler as pictured uses Highland yarn by Harrisville Designs.
- ½ ounce white or natural

> The pattern is available as a download at www.schiffercraft.com/intermediate&advancedpunchneedle.

> For more about using different punch needle sizes and the Craftsman's Punch Needle, see Amy Oxford's companion book *Punch Needle Rug Hooking: Your Complete Resource to Learn & Love the Craft* (pages 131–145).

In a Nutshell

Why use different needle sizes?

- Design: Varying loop height is one of the easiest and most effective ways to create interest and beauty in punch needle rug hooking. A design—whether for the wall or the floor—can be like a relief carving, using high and low areas to make certain elements prominent while others recede.

- Function: What will your punch needle project be used for? Depending on your answer, some needle sizes will work better than others. For example, if I said out loud in a room full of strangers, "I'd rather sit on an 8 than a 10," I would get strange looks for sure. But in the secret language that is Punch Needle Speak, we all know I'm talking about needle size for a chair pad!

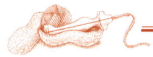

INTRODUCTION

As punch needle rug hooking becomes increasingly popular all across the globe, our choice of tools multiplies. Lucky us! There are punches with adjustable needles, interchangeable needles, and needles fat, skinny, short, and tall. Most needles themselves are metal, but the handles that hold them can be metal, wood, or plastic. Some punches have intricate threading mechanisms or even need a separate threader to guide yarn through the needle channel and into the eye. Others thread with nothing more than a steady hand. The most-popular brands are readily available, so we have no excuse not to try out a few different ones.

If you're in the market for a new tool, you may want to schedule some time on your calendar for an internet "punch needle tool" search. You'll be busy for a while because there are *a lot*.

CHOOSING A PUNCH NEEDLE

To every needle its project, and to every project its needle.

Usually when we think about "different needle size" we're referring to varying loop, or *rug pile*, heights, but the circumference of the needle matters, as well. "Needle size" refers to two measures—(1) the **circumference** of the needle, which determines what thickness of yarn you can use with it, and (2) the **height** of the needle, which determines the height of the loops it makes.

After you've tried out some different needles, likely you'll have one or more favorites, the ones that work best for *your* work: your designs, materials, workspace, and budget. While I am an enthusiastic [*cough*] collector [*cough*] of all kinds of punch needles, I most admire a woman who made huge hooked tapestries with just one tool—the Deluxe Columbia Minerva Rug Needle. Although no longer manufactured, its successors are several generations of what today is sold as the Craftsman's Punch Needle.

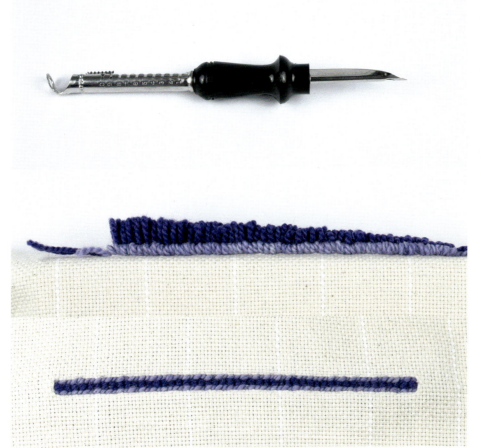

Top: A Craftsman Punch Needle. *Center*: A line showing all 10 loop heights punched in one continuous row (shown from the side). *Bottom*: A party on the front and all business on the back! (The light-purple stitches on either side of the row are punched with an Oxford fine #14 to keep the line of loops orderly, kind of like the bouncers at said party.)

Here's a close look at two of the most versatile punch needle brands, the Craftsman mentioned above and the Oxford Punch Needle.

CRAFTSMAN'S PUNCH NEEDLE

The Craftsman is an adjustable punch needle. The hollow cylindrical needle inside the handle slides up and down and locks into one of 10 numbered notches. The notches determine loop height. For example, notch no. 10 holds the needle in place to make a low pile of just over ¼". Notch number 1 makes a deep pile of just over ¾". It is possible to punch with every single setting without having to stop and cut the yarn and rethread the needle! The Craftsman's Punch Needle can be a time and space saver, and it's fairly easy on crafters' budgets.

But what the Craftsman saves in time, space, and dollars, it lacks in versatility of another kind. It works only with bulky (traditional rug) yarn. The yarn also needs to be fairly smooth because of the Craftsman's design—moving parts and a tricky-to-thread-through locking mechanism. All those novelty yarns and yarn combos that many contemporary rug hookers love to use? They're pretty much off-limits in the Craftsman. It also doesn't make loops less than ¼" tall, which may not scale to designs with a lot of detail, small pieces such as coasters and ornaments, or garments and other wearables that need to be lightweight.

(For more about the Craftsman's Punch Needle and how to use it, see Amy Oxford's companion book *Punch Needle Rug Hooking: Your Complete Resource to Learn & Love the Craft* (pages 131–135).

A complete set of eight Oxford Punch Needles

OXFORD PUNCH NEEDLES

Oxford Punch Needles are available in two needle point sizes and five needle heights. The point size determines how thick or thin of a yarn can thread through the needle. The **height** determines the height of the loops it makes (depth of pile). Altogether there are eight different sizes. Each size is a separate tool.

USING DIFFERENT PUNCH NEEDLE SIZES

Sample loops punched with all eight needle sizes. *Left to right*: #8 fine, #8 regular, #9 fine, #9 regular, #10 fine, #10 regular, #13 fine (the Mini with Heels), and #14 fine (the Mini).

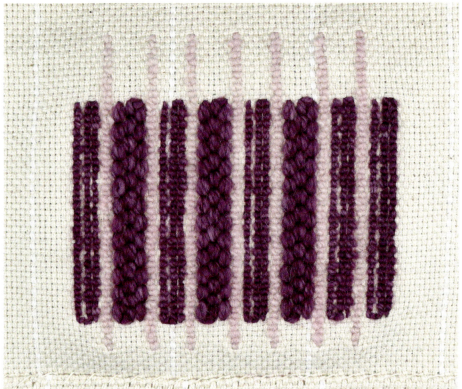

Sample loops from the back

An accurate measure of loops made with the eight Oxford Punch Needle sizes and worsted-weight yarn, one strand for fine point needles and two strands for regular point needles. *Left to right:* #8 fine, #8 regular, #9 fine, #9 regular, #10 fine, #10 regular, #13 fine, and #14 fine.

Oxford punches thread quickly and easily. They also have the advantage of a smooth, clean needle channel, which works well with a variety of novelty yarns and yarn combinations.

Keen readers will have noticed that Oxford Punch Needle sizes 10, 9, and 8 come in both regular and fine point styles. This means they can be paired up to get more detail in a large rug while maintaining consistent pile depth. So, for example, in the big *Texas Cattle Ranch* rug that I have planned, I'm going to use rug yarn and a #9 regular punch for the barn, North Forty, and sky. I'm going to use worsted-weight yarn and a #9 fine for the cowboy, bluebonnets, and chickens. No sacrificing detail to a rug-yarn chicken—with thinner yarn and needle, they can be tiny *and* still look like chickens. I love working this way! It makes so many of my design ideas possible that would not be otherwise.

Oxford Punch Needles come with regular or fine needle points. #9 fine point needle (*left*) and #9 regular point needle (*right*).

Regular point needles use rug yarn or equivalent and are available in sizes 10, 9, and 8. They make loops ¼", ⅜", and ½" high, respectively. The regular point needles (and their predecessors, including the Craftsman) were invented for making rugs with heavyweight wool yarn. They put the "rug" in punch needle!

Fine point needles use worsted-weight yarn or equivalent and are available in sizes 14, 13, 10, 9, and 8. They make loops ⅛", 3/16", ¼", ⅜", and ½", respectively. The size 14 and 13 needles, with their fine points and short lengths, are perfect for making objects that require a low, dense pile without getting heavy. They produce durable handbags, belts, and other accessories. Fine point needles also make beautiful pictures that have the look of needlepoint or woven tapestry.

USING DIFFERENT PUNCH NEEDLE SIZES

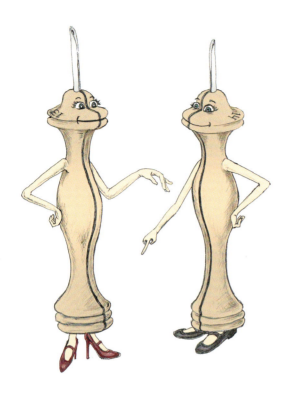

Meet the two Minis. The Mini with Heels (#13 fine) is a tad taller than the Mini (#14 fine). Illustration by Cotey Gallagher.

Embellished Clutch. Oxford Certified Instructor Micah Clasper-Torch, Los Angeles, California. 10" × 6". Oxford fine #13. Wool-acrylic yarn blend.

"This clutch was an opportunity to experiment with novelty yarn and mixing punch needle with other techniques like beading. Working with the fine needles, especially the #13 and #14 fine, creates a less bulky pile height and a more pliable textile that works beautifully for accessories and fashion pieces."

MAKING A SAMPLER

> Sampler: A collection that contains examples of something so that you can get an idea of what it is like.
>
> —*Cambridge Dictionary*

The project in this chapter is a loop-height sampler to make and keep as a reference. In true sampler fashion, it will give you an idea of what it is like to punch with different-sized needles. It will also be nice to have something convincing to show to your family when they ask why you need so many punch needles. Because *this*, you can say, pointing to your sampler.

The sampler demonstrates how loops made with different sizes of punch needles look and feel *and compare to each other*. It will help you choose wisely which needles to use for the things you like to make, from floor rugs so plush that your toes disappear into them, to wall art that looks like it's carved in relief.

The Heart Sampler uses all eight sizes of Oxford Punch Needle and a Craftsman's Punch Needle at settings 6, 7, 8, 9, and 10. It has a little bit of every reason to experiment with different needle sizes, including

- emphasizing or deemphasizing parts of a design
- using regular and fine point needles of the same numbered size to get more detail in a design
- combining different needle sizes with other techniques
- changing loop heights with the Craftsman without rethreading the needle

CHOOSING THE YARN

The single most important factor in the success of your sampler is the yarn you use to make it. The sampler can do its job only if it shows a true and accurate measure of loops that different needle sizes make. The best way to accomplish this is to use the same yarn throughout so that the only variable you're working with is needle size.

Use worsted-weight, smooth-textured, 100% wool yarn: worsted weight so that you can use a single strand in fine point needles and a double strand in regular point needles, smooth textured so that it feeds consistently through the different punch needles, and 100% wool because wool is resilient after steam pressing and it holds up over time—if your loops ever get crushed, you can revive them with a few quick puffs of steam. Worsted-weight wool yarn is readily available and comes in many colors, so you can customize your sampler with colors you love!

Pro Tip: Here are two easy ways to manage yarn when you're switching back and forth between single strand and double strand and you have only one ball or skein of the color. (1) Stranding from both ends of a center-pull ball (shown here) and (2) stranding from both ends of a skein. This method requires a little more patience, but it works well if you don't have a ball winder (or, if you're like me, you would rather spend your time punching instead of winding)!

HEARTS SAMPLER

ABOUT THE PATTERN

STITCH SIZE AND ROW SPACING

Generally speaking, follow standard stitches-per-inch measures: four stitches per inch for two strands of worsted-weight yarn held together (remember that worsted-weight yarn doubled approximates a single strand of rug-weight yarn), and 12 stitches per inch for one strand of worsted-weight yarn. By now you are an accomplished puncher or at least an adventurous novice, so let your experience and acquired instinct guide your stitch and row spacing for a sampler such as this one.

Line drawing on paper.

It's often helpful to color in your pattern to get an idea of what the finished version might look like. This is a "working version," meaning it's mirror-imaged to be a more convenient reference as you work. Each color has a dark, medium, and light value. If you would like to play with the same color concept (4 colors in 3 shades each), choose your 12 yarns and make your own color study. Or use whatever yarn colors you have on hand! Download several copies (see page 42) or make photocopies so you can try coloring in different ways. You can also assign numbers to your colors and write the numbers on the pattern. For example, pink light, medium, and dark could be P1, P2, and P3.

Amy used four colors: pink, olive, dusty blue, and ocher. Each color has a light, medium, and dark value.

A Note from Amy

TAKING ON A DAUNTING PROJECT—IT'S ALL IN THE PLANNING AND THE ATTITUDE!

I've made other basic samplers to show Oxford and Craftsman punch needle sizes, but never anything as complex as the Hearts Sampler. At first glance I felt intimidated, but when I took the time to study the punch size diagram and make my plan of attack, I realized that this would be a really fun challenge, not just for needle sizes but also for color placement.

The planning
By breaking the project down into baby steps, it becomes more doable. My job was to figure out the punch sizes and techniques and to choose four pretty colors and figure out where to put them, knowing that my choices would affect how you saw the hearts and which colors would pop forward and which would recede. I chose soft colors and tried to make sure that all four of my darks were the same *amount* of dark, my reasoning being that really dark areas would dominate. I also tried to keep all four of my light and my four mediums the same values. I didn't pick any bright colors to jump out at me, but that's just me and how I felt on the day (subdued?). I went for subtle, but you could go for dramatic. There's no right or wrong, just different!

I knew I'd have to plan ahead, so I made multiple photocopies of the line drawing and started coloring, trying to get a nice balance of color with my pink, olive blue, and ocher. First, I used my colored pencils faintly to place the colors. Then, when I was happy with that, I began choosing which of the colors to make dark, medium, and light. I kept the light areas faint, and for the mediums I pressed down a bit harder with my pencil, then even harder for my darks. It took several tries to get a look I liked. I chose to do all my bead stitches in light and dark so the dot effect would really show up, and I did the same with the faux plaids.

The attitude
I'm a perfectionist and normally labor over such decisions, trying to get everything just right. I have a reminder note by my desk saying, "It Doesn't Have To Be Perfect!" I decided my colors were pretty enough that I couldn't really go wrong, and that I should lighten up (me, not my colors). Then I lined up my punches with my map at my side, took a deep breath, popped in an audio book, and jumped in. After all, I reminded myself, it's meant to be a sampler, not a masterpiece! The following photos show my punching in progress.

Working Version - Needle Sizes

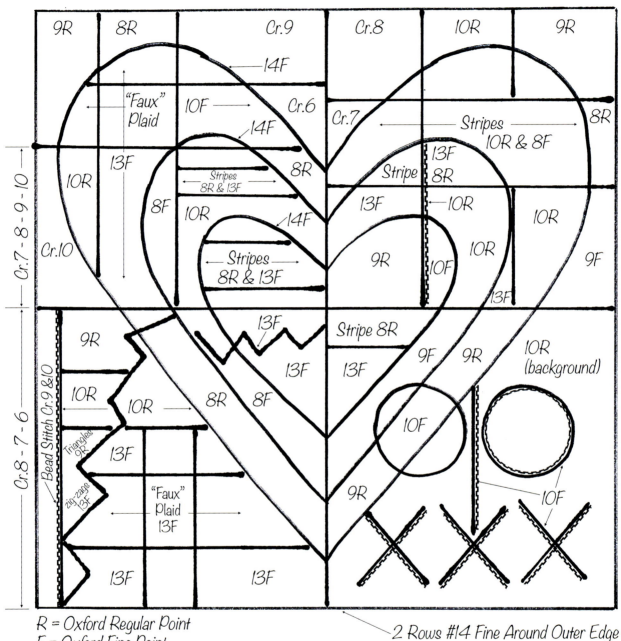

R = Oxford Regular Point
F = Oxford Fine Point
Cr. = Craftsman Punch Needle
〰️ = Bead Stitch

2 Rows #14 Fine Around Outer Edge

This working version of the map shows the punch needle sizes used in the sampler.

Pro Tip: Make multiple photocopies of the blank map so you don't have to worry about getting it right the first time!

Here are five specific ways to use different needle sizes in punch needle rug hooking, *and why*. All five are used in the Hearts Sampler.

1. **Emphasizing or deemphasizing parts of a design**: Use an Oxford fine #10 to outline the hearts with white or natural yarn. These are the shortest loops in the entire sampler. They will nearly disappear into the background.

2. **Using fine and regular point needles of the same numbered size to get more detail**: Use an Oxford fine #10 to punch the fine lines—the Xs, circle, and vertical line. Use an Oxford regular #10 to fill in the background.

3. **Combining different needle sizes with other punching techniques: Bead stitch:** using a Craftsman needle set at 9 and 10 (make bead stitch where vertical and horizontal lines intersect). **Stripes:** using Oxford regular #10 and fine #8. **"Faux" plaid:** using Oxford fines #10 and #13.

4. **Changing loop height without rethreading the needle** (Craftsman only)

5. **Use every needle size in your sampler somewhere in the border.** That way, when you turn your sampler over (after hemming), you'll have an example of all the heights to compare.

Pro Tip: Take an extra-fine-point Sharpie and darken the punch needle sizes stamped on the bottom of your punches. This will make the sizes easier to read and speed up the punching process. Some punchers also write the sizes on the handles. If you have the complete set of eight Oxford Punch Needles, you could write or embroider the sizes on the bag.

LET'S PUNCH!

For this project, Amy punched in the following order:

1. outline of hearts
2. border section made with Craftsman's Punch Needle
3. single lines
4. bead stitch (For bead stitch directions, see chapter 6.)
5. stripes
6. faux plaids
7. everything else

Use an Oxford fine #14 to outline the hearts with white or natural yarn. These are the shortest loops in the sampler, and I wanted the outlines to nearly disappear into the background.

Each one of these sections of border (shown from the front) was punched using the Craftsman *without* rethreading the needle. The green color loops were made at settings 10, 9, 8, and 7, about four stitches per setting. If you look closely you can see the "steps." The rest of the green loops were made at settings 6, 7, and 8. For more about working with the Craftsman's Punch Needle, see Amy Oxford's companion book *Punch Needle Rug Hooking: Your Complete Resource to Learn & Love the Craft* (pages 131–135).

The setting 6 loops are the highest in the entire sampler. Change the setting when your needle is all the way down in the monk's cloth: unlock the needle, slide it to another notch, and lock it in place. Do this while working on the back. In other words, punch along until you want to change the height, keep your needle all the way down in your backing, change the setting without snipping or poking, and then carry on punching. A bit fiddly for sure, but a good technique to know.

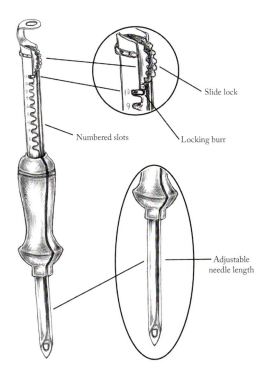

The Craftsman's Punch Needle. **Caution:** Do not pinch the lock! If you do, it will be too small and keep falling out!

USING DIFFERENT PUNCH NEEDLE SIZES

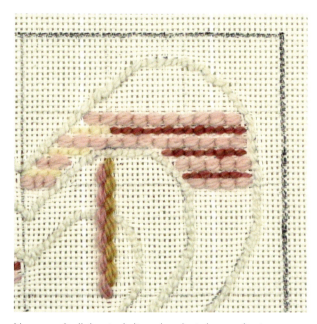

Next punch all the single lines, bead stitches, and stripes.

Single lines, bead stitch, and stripes shown from the front. When punching stripes, stop at the end of each row as opposed to going back and forth. This will leave ends to be trimmed later. Leave the ends on the long side (approximately ½") to make it easy to keep track of them. Make sure to trim the ends the same height as the loops!

A WORD ABOUT PLAID

In *Puzzle of Love* (page 40), Louise experimented with a technique she named "faux plaid." In the Hearts Sampler, faux plaid is made like this: Punch vertical rows of blue with an Oxford fine #13, leaving an empty row of monk's cloth between each row. Punch horizontal rows of pink with an Oxford fine #10, again leaving an empty row of monk's cloth between each row.

Where pink intersects blue, punch into the empty holes left between the blue rows. This means, of course, that pink jumps over blue, creating slightly raised bumps on the back. Since this sampler is a reference tool to help choose needle sizes for future projects, there is no concern about an uneven underside causing premature wear. Would you use faux plaid all over a floor rug? Probably not if you cared about its longevity.

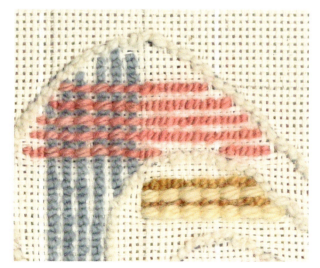

Close-up of plaid (back)

All the plaids are now completed (front).

"Everything else" has now been filled in (shown on back). Two rows of light pink were added around the outside using Oxford fine #14.

Pro Tip: Be careful not to overpack! If you do, your bead stitches won't look like a dotted line, and your plaids will be a messy jumble. You want your loops to have room to "bloom" and not be all squished together like too many people on a subway.

USING DIFFERENT PUNCH NEEDLE SIZES 57

Completed Hearts Sampler (front), steam-pressed and finished with whipping. Amy reports, "This sampler really did feel like doing a puzzle. When I punched that last little shape, I had the same sense of satisfaction I feel when I put in that last piece of a jigsaw puzzle! It was a great way to test out all the punches, and I *loved* making plaids!"

Pro Tips:

- Snipping and poking as you go. The Hearts Sampler requires lots of snipping and poking because there are so many small details. If you do this as you go, it will be easier than waiting until the end.

- Checking the front often. With something this intricate, it's important to keep an eye on the prize (the front). Turn your work to the front as you work on each area to make sure you're getting the effect that you want.

- Taking notes. Write down what needle sizes, loop heights, tools, and techniques you like and which ones you never want to do again!

- Clipping yarn tails. You'll be cutting lots of yarn ends that are adjacent to loops and other ends of other heights. Ensure that your ends are the same size as the loops they belong to by poising your bent-handled scissors *lightly* atop the row when you clip.

- Adjusting loops. Sometimes if you adjust your loops a little too enthusiastically with your pointy embroidery scissors, you can have an *incident*—the sides of the blades could cut into the wool. Avoid this mishap by threading a knitting needle into loops to pull up on and align them.

- Filling holidays. You can fill in rug yarn holidays neatly and with less bulk by using a corresponding size of fine point punch needle and matching worsted-weight yarn.

- Avoiding "punch-throughs." If your loops start to crowd, reach underneath with your nondominant hand and push existing loops out of the way.

Figure 1

STEAM-PRESSING AND HEMMING THE SAMPLER

1. Place your sampler *with the backside facing up* on top of several layers of thick terry towel. The loops need something soft to sink into. (They'll think they're at the spa).

2. Steam-press as usual.

3. Turn the sampler over to the front and *immediately*—while it is still steamy and very wet—use your hands and fingers to push and pinch the loops to their true heights.

4. You also can use a knitting needle to reinforce shapes, especially the mostly hidden heart outlines punched at the very beginning (figure 1). This can make a dramatic difference with the definition of your colors and shapes. This technique is especially helpful for lining up the rows in the plaids.

5. Let your sampler dry thoroughly before handling it.

6. You can go over your sampler with a sweater depiller, but if you do, be sure to use a light touch!

7. You can hem your sampler with the usual 2" folded monk's cloth hem or whip stitch as pictured.

> For more about steam pressing and hemming, see Amy Oxford's companion book *Punch Needle Rug Hooking: Your Complete Resource to Learn & Love the Craft* (pages 123–130).

USING DIFFERENT PUNCH NEEDLE SIZES

SIMPLIFIED HEARTS SAMPLER

Simplified Hearts Sampler, 8" × 8" (front).

Amy reports, "I really enjoyed making the Hearts Sampler and had leftover yarn so I thought I'd create a simplified version that used only Oxford Punch Needles with larger areas to fill in. In choosing what punch size to use for the new heart, I thought of the phrases 'my heart sank' (as in something dreadful happened) versus 'my heart soared' (as in something wonderful happened). The Valentine's Day cynic in me was tempted to make a sunken heart (after all, it would look great), but the romantic in me won out and I decided to go with heart soaring, with the heart taller than its background. I had fun punching this piece and seeing how the different punch needle heights looked side by side. Mostly, though, I just wanted an excuse to punch more plaid! Leave it to my creative friend Louise to figure out how to punch plaid!"

Simplified Hearts Sampler Pattern, working version (backward)

Pattern size: 8" × 8"

You will need:

- Monk's cloth size: 20" × 20" or size needed to fit your frame
- 10" × 10" or 14" × 14" Oxford Gripper Strip Lap Frame
- Oxford Punch Needles #8, #9, and #10 regular point
- Oxford Punch Needles #8, #9, #10, #13, and #14 fine point
- A stitch gauge
- Small, sharp embroidery scissors

Yarn needed:

- 100% wool worsted-weight yarn for all of sampler. Amy used Harrisville Designs Highland brand yarn worked with single strands for the fine point Oxford Punch Needles and double strands for the regular point Oxford Punch Needles.
- Approximately 5 ounces total in your choice of several colors. Amy used four colors: pink, olive, dusty blue, and ocher. Pink, olive, and dusty blue have a light, a medium, and a dark value. Ocher has only a medium and light value. This pattern is a wonderful way to use up leftover yarns.
- 1 ounce white or natural

The same basic directions used for the Hearts Sampler apply to the Simplified version as well.

The pattern is available as a download at www.schiffercraft.com/intermediate&advancedpunchneedle.

Working Version - Needle Sizes

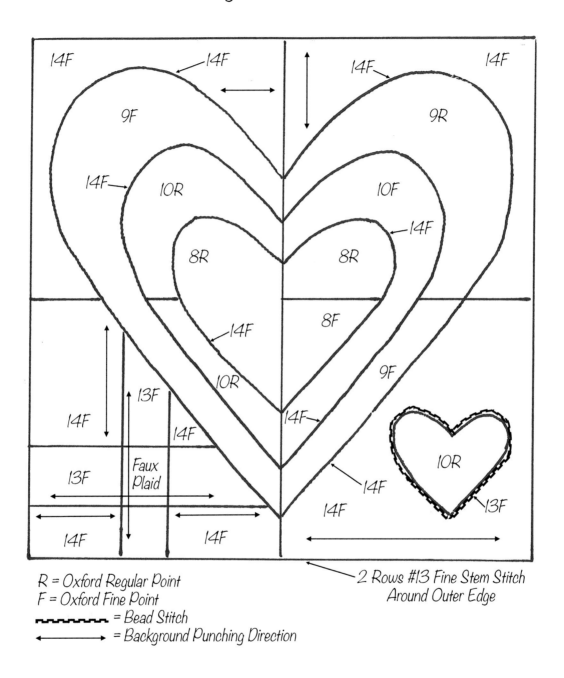

Punch needle size chart for Simplified Hearts Sampler. This is a "working version" (backward). Download several copies (see page 61) or make photocopies so you can try multiple color combinations.

Finished Simplified Hearts Sampler (back)

. A Note from Amy .

WHAT I LEARNED FROM MAKING LOUISE'S HEARTS SAMPLER AND MY SIMPLIFIED HEARTS SAMPLER

- I learned that I *love* making "faux" plaid! Especially with the Oxford fine #13. It took a bit of time to poke all the loops into place at the end, but I didn't mind because the result was so satisfying!

- Using a thin knitting needle and laying it sideways to separate areas was a *huge* game changer for me. It cleaned up edges better than I ever have before. Better than poking alone. The combination of poking individual loops into place and then separating areas with the knitting needle gave excellent definition and really helped get the rows of plaid to line up properly.

- After *never* jumping over other loops (well . . . maybe once or twice), it was liberating to jump while making plaid. I felt like a punch needle rebel *with* a cause. I agree with Louise that I probably wouldn't use this technique on a floor rug (due to the risk of slightly taller "jumping stitches" pulling out), but plaid could be such fun in other punched pieces!

USING DIFFERENT PUNCH NEEDLE SIZES

Geometric Tone-on-Tone. Advanced Oxford Certified Instructor Kim Scanlan, St. Paul, Minnesota. 12" × 12". Oxford regular #8, #9, and #10 with wool rug yarn and Oxford fine #13 and #14 with worsted-weight rug yarn. The middle diamond has been sculpted.

"I wanted to create a geometric piece that highlighted how using different punch needles can create depth and texture in a piece. Using the same color of rug and worsted-weight yarn allows the design to speak for itself without distractions of color combinations."

Rush Rug. Advanced Oxford Certified Instructor Cotey Gallagher, Salisbury, Vermont. 60" × 60". Wool rug yarn alternating every two rows between Oxford regular #9 and regular #10.

"This was given as a housewarming gift to a friend and fellow music lover. I asked them what their all-time favorite album was, and I researched what its colors were from the original vinyl record. I learned a great deal from this piece, and if I made another, I would begin in the center to keep the roundness of the rug from skewing."

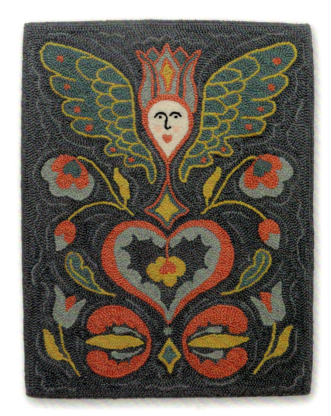

Folk Angel Fraktur. Oxford Certified Instructor Katie Stackhouse, Calgary, Alberta, Canada. 22" × 28". Hand-dyed wool rug yarn using Oxford regular #10 (background), regular #9 (foreground), and fine #9 (face).

"This fraktur rug is inspired by Pennsylvania Dutch bookplates from the 1830s. By using contrasting punch needle sizes, I was able to create a subtle sense of depth as the background recedes slightly from the higher elements in the foreground."

Figs. Advanced Oxford Certified Instructor Kelly Wright, Icking, Bavaria, Germany. 12" × 12". This piece incorporates fine shading (figs), background shading (7 shades of gold), and multiple needle sizes: Oxford fine #14 (figs and background) and fine #13 (border). Twelve stitches per inch were used throughout.

"I used worsted-weight wool and Oxford fine #13 and #14 to replicate shading in the style of a still life. The border contrasts starkly and employs stitching in every hole."

Champlain Valley Map. Oxford Certified Instructor Kris Andrews, Middlebury, Vermont. 12" × 48". Oxford fine #14 (cities, towns, and fields) and fine #9, #13, and #14 (forests and mountains).

"This was inspired by raised relief maps and Catherine Jordan's maps, which combine embroidery and painted fabric. The lake is painted with Jacquard textile paint. For the land, I used varied punch needle heights to create a tactile topographic effect."

Ode to Christmas Walks. Oxford Certified Instructor Michelle O Driscoll, Cork, Munster, Ireland. 24" × 48". Punched with wool yarn and Irish Aran-weight yarn in both single and doubled strands, using Oxford regular #9, #10, and #13 and fine #9 and #10.

"This rug was started on New Year's Day 2020 and finished during the first Covid lockdown. Each year since my kids were babies, we go on 'Christmas Walks' during the Christmas holidays. We put on our wellies and go out the doors and walk fields for miles and miles. It's a real adventure; we climb ditches and hedges, cross streams, climb over fallen trees, and celebrate our wonderful creatures."

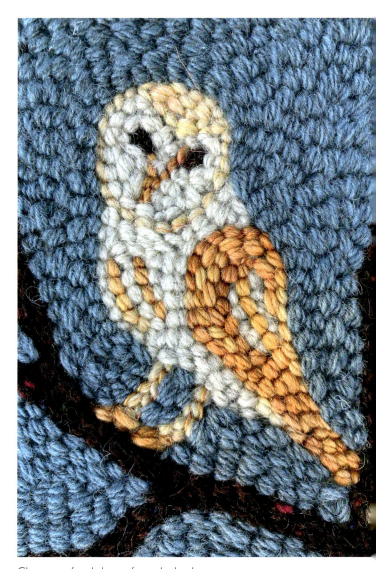

Close-up of owl shown from the back.

Friendship Padula Pillow. Oxford Certified Instructor Rebecca Martin, Longmont, Colorado. 15" × 15". In this piece Rebecca has used an effect we call "reverse punching": you punch on the front of the rug instead of the back to create flat stitches. In Rebecca's pillow, the background is reverse punching (loop side down) and the main motifs are regular punching (loop side up). Both sides are punched with an Oxford regular #10 and hand-dyed rug-weight yarn.

"A woman came by my studio to get rug yarn to finish a project she had started before the pandemic. We had never met before, but within minutes on the porch we connected. After weeks of isolation, my first visitor renewed a spark in me as we shared different creative ideas with each other. A friendship and a rug design were born."

Amy's note: The term *padula* was coined by the famous traditional rug hooker Pearl McGown to describe any stylized flower that is not recognizable as a specific species.

3
Sculpting

by Louise Kulp with contributions by Amy Oxford

THE SWEATER LETTER PROJECT

Louise Kulp. *Sweater Letter*. 9.75 × 9.25". Wool on cotton.

This project uses worsted-weight yarn and Oxford fine point punch needle sizes #8, #9, #10, #13, and #14.

Pattern size: 8.5" × 8.5"

You will need:

- Monk's cloth size: 18" × 18" or size needed to fit your frame
- 10" × 10" or 14" × 14" Oxford Gripper Strip Lap Frame. You will be doing a lot of work on the front (public) side of the work, cutting and sculpting your loops. Both frames will work, but the 14" × 14" will give you more room to maneuver on the front side.
- Oxford fine point punch needle sizes #8, #9, #10, #13, and #14 (*Note: It is possible to make this project with just one needle if you regulate the length of the loops by hand. Use a fine point punch needle equivalent to size 14 or 13—⅛" and ³⁄₁₆" high loops, respectively.*)
- Small, sharp embroidery scissors
- Optional: 10" square of felt and matching sewing or embroidery thread to back the project

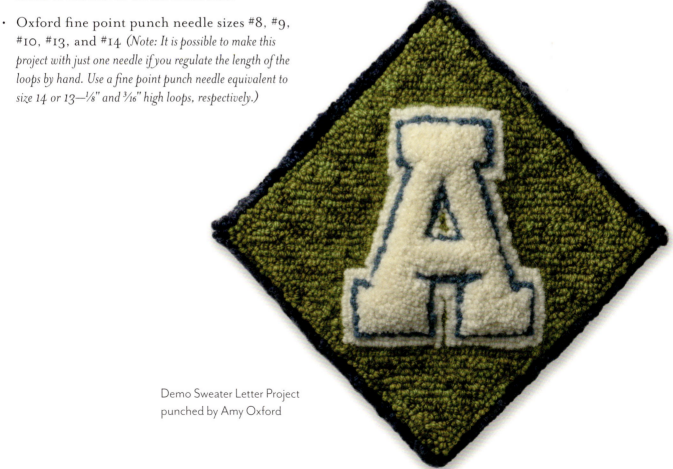

Demo Sweater Letter Project punched by Amy Oxford

Tool Box

There are several special tools that make sculpting easier. If they're not already in your rug hooking bag, they're probably somewhere else around your house!

1. To brush away sculpting fuzz, I recommend a kitchen "scrubby" made of netting OR
2. A nail brush with soft plastic bristles OR
3. A nail brush with soft natural bristles
4. A thin knitting needle
5. Tweezers to pull out errant clipped stitches
6. Clover-brand Jumbo Tapestry Needle with blunt point to align loops before cutting
7. Bent-handled scissors (also called machine embroidery scissors) for precise shaping

Yarn needed:

Four colors of 100% wool worsted-weight yarn.

- **Letter**—white: 1 ounce
- **Letter Outline**—turquoise-blue medium: 0.5 ounces
- **Background**—Violet Jane worsted-weight "In a Pickle" green for the demo project: 1 ounce
- **Outer Border**—navy blue: 0.3 ounces

In a Nutshell

- The sculpting technique is used to create three-dimensional effects in rug hooking. Loops are punched in rows of graduated heights and then clipped (cut open) and shaped (sculpted) to make motifs that are higher than the flat-hooked background.

- The loops are punched *very densely* so that when clipped and sheared, they produce a thick, lush pile that looks and feels like velvet.

- Traditionally, sculpting is reserved for motifs that the artist wants to be "stars of the show"—a beautiful red rose in the center of a rug, for example.

- What is the difference between **Sculpting** and chapter 2's technique **Using Different Needle Sizes**? After all, they both use multiple needle sizes within a single design. Sculpting is punching deliberately graduated rows of loops that get cut open and "carved" into three-dimensional shapes. The other technique is making loops of all different heights, either randomly or in planned-out schemes, to add texture and interest to a design.

INTRODUCTION

Punch needle rug hookers may want to take inspiration from the historical Waldoboro style of sculpted (or "sculptured") hand-hooked rugs. The style was developed during the second half of the 19th century in the Broad Bay area of Maine, which includes the town of Waldoboro. Jacqueline Hansen is an expert Waldoboro style designer, teacher, and historian. Her book, *Sculptured Rugs in Waldoboro Style* (Rug Hooking Magazine, 2007), is about the history of the tradition. It includes many photos of her own rugs, as well as those of her students and other contemporary fiber artists who incorporate the Waldoboro legacy into their work.

Back in 19th-century Broad Bay, there were certain motifs that appeared frequently in sculpted rugs. Blueberries, strawberries, the distinctive red "Waldoboro rose," and daisies were often given star treatment. Such motifs naturally lent themselves to sculpting and were the centers of attention literally, since they often were placed in the middle of a pattern, surrounded by a border of scrolls.

While fruits and flowers were the norm in the 19th century, 21st-century rug hookers who sculpt the Waldoboro way adapt the tradition to suit their own styles. They are expanding the catalog of motifs to include birds (and their eggs, and their nests), pets, seashells, trees, surf, clouds, geometric shapes, abstract shapes, words and letters, mountains, architecture . . . in other words, almost anything!

PUNCH NEEDLE RUG HOOKING AND SCULPTING

Traditional sculpted rugs usually are hooked with fine cuts of wool, which give the clipped and shaped parts a rich, refined appearance. To achieve the same richness in the project for this chapter, we'll use worsted-weight yarn, which is comparable to 3-cut (³⁄₃₂" wide) strips. Our sweater letter will take on the look and feel of chenille, the very material used to make vintage varsity letters!

While it's possible to sculpt with rug-weight yarn, the clipped and shaped areas won't be as refined, and you won't be able to fit as many different-sized rows into the same size space.

Cotey Gallagher sculpted the entire surface of her 40" × 20" rug titled *Melted Sherbet*. Why shape just a few flavors when you can shape them all? Although Cotey has not cut her loops, she has definitely achieved a sculpted effect.

Melted Sherbet. Advanced Oxford Certified Instructor Cotey Gallagher, Salisbury, Vermont. 40" × 20". Rug-weight wool yarn, Oxford regulars #8, 9, and 10, and Craftsman settings 1–7, with setting 1 creating the tallest loops in the centers of the sculpted shapes.

"This is a free-form-drawn rug sculpted by using multiple needle heights of Oxford Punch Needles and the Craftsman's Punch Needle. Mock shading is used to create the illusion of extra depth." (See chapter 4 for more on mock shading.)

SCULPTING 77

BEGINNING THE PROJECT

Our Sweater Letter Project has quite the retro vibe, but it's a decidedly modern interpretation of the sculpturing technique developed and practiced by creative hooking artists in 19th-century Broad Bay.

Choose your letter from our "varsity" alphabet patterns. I started at the beginning of the alphabet with "A," so for me, it's one down and 25 to go! Probably you don't want to make that big of a commitment, but maybe you'd like to sculpt your initial, or spell out your baby nephew's name in colors to match his nursery, or make a celebratory banner for a newly married couple.

Enlarge the letter to your desired size. The "A" is 4½" tall and fits nicely into an 8½" high × 8½" wide diamond-shaped background. Trace it onto monk's cloth. The letter "A" is symmetrical, so there is no need to trace it backward. But for B, C, D, E, F, G, and so on, obviously there is! Be mindful as you plan your project.

(A note from Amy: To draw your border, grab your 6" square template—or make one if you haven't already, because they sure do come in handy! Turn it 45° and it becomes an 8½" high and wide diamond shape that frames your letter perfectly. Note that the outside border is drawn on the diagonal. The background of the letter will be punched in horizontal rows; more on that later.)

The inside of the letter—the three-dimensional "puffy" part—will be clipped (cut open) and shaped (sculpted). To achieve the dense, velvety pile that sculpting is known for, we'll punch in *every hole* of monk's cloth.

For our varsity letters we have used the font Emilio 20 by Adien Gunarta. The full alphabet is available as a download at www.schiffercraft.com/intermediate&advancedpunchneedle.

PUNCH NEEDLES FOR SCULPTING

The Sweater Letter Project uses all five sizes of Oxford fine point punch needles (8, 9, 10, 13, and 14), *BUT* it is possible to make your Sweater Letter with just one. Choose a #13 or #14 (or equivalent size in another brand) and use it "as is" to punch the background and the three non-sculpted rows around the letter. You can use it for the sculpted area as well, but you'll have to size the loops manually. Lengthen each loop by pulling on it from underneath your frame. This sounds tedious—and it is!—but our project is small, and with practice you'll get pretty consistent. You need only to end up with rows of graduated loop heights precise enough to be sculpted as described below.

The highest point of our letter hits at the center of the puffy part. We'll punch our way in from the left and right edges simultaneously toward the center to achieve what ultimately will be a smoothly rounded and symmetrical mound in the shape of an "A." Think of it as climbing up one side of a mountain and then going back down the other side. **Figure 1** is a topographic map of the concept. You can see that the "A" shape is filled with concentric rounds of closed contours, punched with these needle sizes in this order: 10-9-8-9-10. The thickest parts of the letter (the head and two feet) are filled up with additional rows of #8 loops. We'll clip every row as it's completed. It is much easier to make accurate and complete cuts if you clip as you go. (Diagrams by Louise Kulp and Cotey Gallagher.)

SCULPTING   79

Figure 1: Topographic Map

Figure 2: Color & Needle Size Map

Color and Needle Size Map. This map shows where to place your colors and what size of punch needles to use for each area.

SCULPTING 81

Steps 1, 2, and 3 (back of the letter)

Steps 1, 2, and 3 (front of the letter)

STEP-BY-STEP PUNCHING

STEP 1.

Use an Oxford fine #13.

Note that there are three drawn lines for the outer border and inner triangle. Punch on the middle line with turquoise blue medium on the outer border and inner triangle.

Outline the outer border of the letter with two rows of White. Punch one row of White in the center triangle.

For the first row of white, punch right next to the Turquoise Blue Medium row *without leaving an empty row between.*

For the second row of white, *leave an empty row between.*

These rows will not be sculpted. These are the only #13 loops in the entire project.

STEP 2.

Use an Oxford fine #14.

Punch one row of background color green all around the outside of the letter shape. Leave an empty row between the Green and the White. We'll fill in the rest of the background later.

Fill in the center of the inner triangle with Green.

STEP 3.

Use an Oxford fine #10.

The inside of the letter is punched with White. Punch all around the inside of the letter. Punch right next to the Turquoise Blue Medium row *without leaving an empty row between*. These are the first loops that will be clipped, and the only #10 loops in the entire project.

STEP 4.

Cut open all the #10 loops, but align them first. Use a jumbo tapestry needle to align loops, passing it through a few at a time. If you don't have a large tapestry needle, you can use a short, thin, double-pointed knitting needle or any other smooth tool that slips easily through the middles of loops (4a). Coax them into a straight line, pull them up to full height, and then cut right through the centers with fine point embroidery scissors (4b). Make sure to cut each loop completely open. Repeat this process until you've clipped every single loop in the row. (4c). Note that the loops are cut but NOT the long ends where we've stopped and started. Wait to clip those until they are surrounded by loops, to make sure they are clipped at the right height.

Pro Tip: For this project, and for most sculpting, it's important to clip as you go. It's tempting to do all the punching first and then clip afterward, but if you do, the loops will intermingle, making it really hard to sculpt them well.

4a

4b

4c

5a

5b

STEP 5.

Use an Oxford fine #9.

Punch one row around the "A" shape right next to the #10 row (5a). As you make this row, reach underneath your frame with your nondominant hand and use a finger to push aside and out of the way the clipped ends of the first row. Align and clip open the #9 loops as described in step 4 (5b). These are the only #9 loops in the entire project.

STEP 6.

Use an Oxford fine #8.

Punch one row around the "A" shape right next to the #9 row (6a). Clip open the #8 loops (6b).

STEP 7.

Fill in remaining empty spaces with #8 loops (7a). These will be the spaces at the thickest parts of the letter (the head and feet). Remember to stitch in every hole of monk's cloth. Clip all the remaining loops (7b).

6a

6b

7a

7b

Pro Tip: Take your pattern off the frame after punching and put it back on with the loopy side facing you. This gives you great access to your work for the final stage of sculpting. Stretch it taut as usual.

STEP 8.

Probably you have noticed that the further along you get in your project, the harder it is to maneuver around the inside of your gripper strip frame, if that's what you're using. The challenge is not as great if your piece is stretched on a carpet tack frame or in a sturdy hoop. Those types tend to be shallow, while gripper strip frames are deep. The work area gets cramped and it's harder to align and cut loops with precision. At this point in the project—after the inside of the letter shape is completely filled with loops—pull it off your frame, flip it over, and put it back on with the front side up (shown here). This makes it much easier to finish up any remaining loop cutting, remedy obvious punch-throughs (high loops punched close together = inevitable intermingling), and check for partially clipped stitches. It also will be easier to sculpt your letter from here, so leave things right where they are for now. Note that some punchers prefer to do their loop cutting with their work off the frame.

SCULPTING 85

SCULPTING

Waldoboro-style sculpting can take many forms. A flower petal, for example, is best modeled to represent the way it grows: lowest loops at the base and highest loops at the outer edge. Our Sweater Letter, on the other hand, is sculpted into a symmetrical mound, reflecting its inspiration, the vintage varsity letter.

Before you begin sculpting, use scissors to snip off the *very* tops of yarns ends—don't alter height just yet! Skimming off the top removes a lot of extraneous fluff that would interfere with shaping.

Shape, or sculpt, your letter. Begin at the base of the letter where the #10 loops are, shape up to the top where the #8 loops are, and then back down the other side (Remember our mountain analogy?). Use bent-handled scissors and proceed with patience. Hold your scissors parallel to the row but at a slight angle so that you essentially are cutting beveled edges. This helps avoid leaving steps or "shelves" between row heights as you sculpt.

Work all around your letter and evaluate its shape constantly. Hold it at eye level and look at it from all 360°. *You can always trim away a little bit more, but you cannot undo overzealous scissor work!* Keep your eye on the prize: a nicely rounded and symmetrical mound in the shape of your letter. Strive for a smooth, undetectable transition from one row height to the next.

Pro Tip: If you need to make a course correction after you've cut loops open, use tweezers to pull out one stitch at a time from the back.

When you're satisfied with your sculpting, having checked it every which way many times over, you can punch your border and background. (If you turned your project front side up to do the sculpting, return it to backside up to do the background.)

Border: Punch 2 rows around the outside edge of your diamond, using Navy Blue yarn and an Oxford fine #14.

Background: In step 1 we punched one row of background around the letter with Green yarn and an Oxford fine #14. Fill in the rest with the same color and punch size. I stitched the background with horizontal rows to resemble knitting, the fabric of vintage varsity knitwear. (I love it when textile techniques reference each other!)

Use your kitchen scrubby, nail brush, or a piece of gathered tulle to brush away sculpting debris as you go (just like Michelangelo kept all of that pesky marble dust under control).

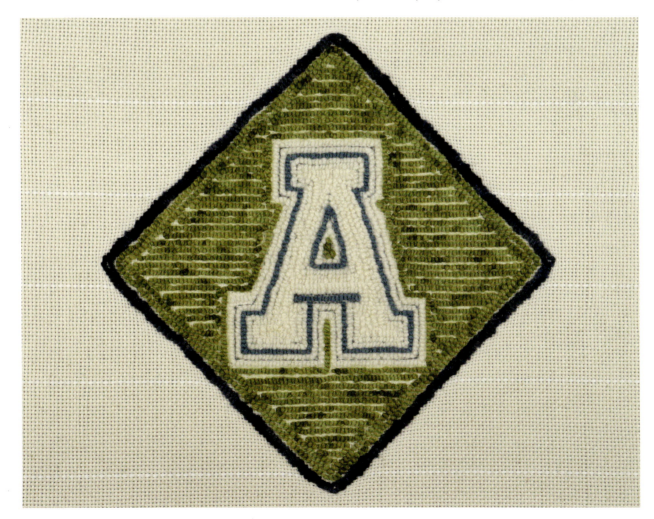

FINISHING

Caution! Be sure to follow these steam-pressing directions carefully—you don't want to squish your beautiful letter!

Steam-press your letter. First, press the back. Ready a cold water-soaked towel and a dry iron with the dial set at "Wool." Put your project *front side down* on top of several layers of terry cloth towel, and steam the sculpted part of the letter. Apply slight pressure only!—you don't want to crush the beautiful, velvety pile.

Turn the project over and place it *front side up* on the toweling. Steam the border and background, and the three unclipped #13-punched rows around the outside of the letter; in other words, everywhere except the sculpted part. Steam these flat sections as you normally do, by putting pressure on the iron and holding it down while you count to 10 or 12.

To remove any last fuzz on your letter, brush back and forth gently with your tulle or scrubby. Fine-tune if needed with your scissors. You can use a sweater depiller to brighten up the background, but don't use it on your sculpting.

Amy's finished Sweater Letter

If you plan to make your letter part of a banner or hang it "clothesline style" from an art cable, it's nice to finish it off with a backing of felt or other fabric. I used inexpensive craft-store felt sewn on with perle cotton. Use whip stitch or, for a more decorative look, blanket stitch.

Louise finished her project by backing it with felt that she attached with a decorative blanket stitch. Amy finished hers with a standard 1" hem.

THE SHAPED BUTTERFLY MAT: SCULPTING WITH RUG YARN

Louise Kulp, *Shaped Butterfly Mat*. 7" × 6.5". Wool on cotton.

Sculpting with rug or bulky-weight yarn gives just as beautiful results as sculpting with thinner, worsted-weight yarn. The Shaped Butterfly Mat shown here uses rug yarn punched in six different loop heights. The mildly variegated yarns, when clipped, give the butterfly a soft and natural sculpted surface. Late-19th-century butterfly illustrations inspired the design's muted colors and interesting markings.

You will need:

- Monk's cloth size: 15" × 15" or size needed to fit your frame
- 10" × 10" Oxford Gripper Strip Lap Frame
- Craftsman's Punch Needle
- Oxford regular Punch Needles sizes #8, #9, and #10
- Small, sharp embroidery scissors
- Bent-handled scissors

Yarn needed:

- Five colors of 100% wool rug yarn. Using mildly variegated colors will give you a softer look.

The tallest loops in the design are along the outside edges of the wings. The loops gradually decrease in height from left to right (or right to left, depending on which side of the butterfly you're working!) until the shortest ones fall along the inside edges of the wings where they meet the butterfly body.

The two upper wings were punched with Craftsman settings 5, 6, and 7 (outside edge to inside edge, respectively). The two lower wings were punched with Oxford regular #8, #9, and #10 (outside edge to inside edge, respectively). Using a sequence of taller loops for the top wings and a sequence of shorter loops for the bottom ones gives the illusion that the upper wings overlap the lower.

The design has both linear and round(ish) shapes and was "directional-punched" accordingly; that is, back and forth in rows or outline and fill following a contour. Notice that *each shape has its own needle size / loop height*, unlike the Sweater Letter Project, which uses *multiple loop heights within a single shape*. I completed my butterfly with a delicate whip stitch.

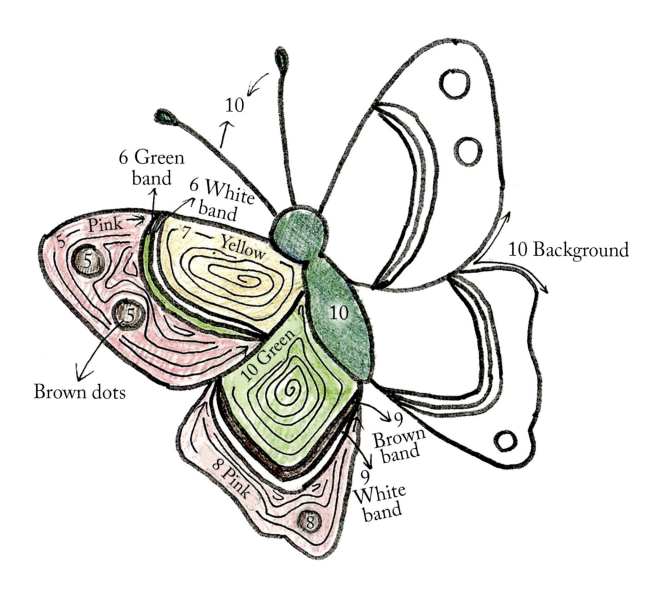

SCULPTING 91

Shaped Butterfly Mat from the back, showing stitch size and row spacing. I decided to whip my mat for a tidy finish that would complement the design and technique. For whipping directions, see Amy Oxford's companion book *Punch Needle Rug Hooking: Your Complete Resource to Learn & Love the Craft* (pages 163–164).

Almost all the "rules" for sculpting with worsted-weight yarn apply to sculpting with rug-weight yarn. The exceptions are stitch size and row spacing. When you're sculpting with bulky yarn, use the Oxford stitch gauge standards: single lines and outlines have six stitches per inch, filling in has four stitches per inch, and there are seven rows per inch. Keeping to these standards will prevent your project from getting so jam packed with yarn that it will live in a permanent state of "puff" no matter how enthusiastically you steam it!

One of the best things about the punch needle technique of rug hooking is its flexibility. For a sculpting project you can use a separate tool for each loop height, *or* use one needle with adjustable settings, *or* coerce a needle into adjustability by hand, pulling loops to their desired lengths, *or* use any combination of the above! Of course, it's faster and easier to have one needle size or setting per loop height, but it's not *necessary*. If you want or need to make a sculpting project with just one punch needle, choose the size that makes the shortest loop in your design (for the Shaped Butterfly Mat, that's a regular #10) and hand-pull all the other loops longer. You'll be clipping and sculpting the loops anyway, so absolute precision is not required at the punching stage. With practice, your trained eyes and hands will become more-accurate "loop sizers." Save precision for clipping and sculpting!

· A Note from Amy ·

WHAT I LEARNED FROM MAKING LOUISE'S SWEATER LETTER PROJECT

I had done some loop clipping and sculpting with rug yarn but never with worsted-weight yarn, such densely packed loops, and the short little loops made by the Oxford fine #13. With this project I learned the following:

- It's scary cutting such teensy little loops open! Breathing helps—yes, I forgot to breathe . . .

- Using the knitting needle to straighten loops before cutting makes the cutting *so* much easier, thus allowing me to breathe!

- I prefer cutting loops open with my embroidery scissors instead of bent-handled scissors. The smaller size made them easier for me to maneuver.

- Before this project, I waited to cut my loops until all the punching was done, and I always had tons of loop-overs (loops punching through and splitting other loops). With Louise's method of cutting after each row, all of my previously punched loops were already cut, so there were no loops to punch through—brilliant!

- I found it easier to sculpt with my work in my hands instead of on the frame. Louise suggests this as an option, and for me, being able to "bend" the work to get a better angle for clipping was just the ticket.

- Laying a knitting needle sideways between the rows created crisp definition for my letter outline (a trick I learned from Louise in chapter 2).

I think my letter would look cool sewn to the back of my jean jacket.

A Burger Coaster Set. Oxford Certified Instructor Kris Andrews, Middlebury, Vermont. 4" × 4". Oxford regular #10, Oxford fine #13 and #14, and Craftsman settings 4–10. Wool rug yarn, wool rug yarn divided into single ply, and worsted-weight wool yarn.

"I enjoy making things that are functional and embody a sense of whimsy. These coasters make me smile. This is just a sampling of the burger toppings and sides, made with a variety of techniques in this collection."

Tribute to Hilma af Klint. Advanced Oxford Certified Instructor Kelly Wright, Bavaria, Germany. 12" × 12". Oxford regular #8, #9, and #10; Oxford fine #8, #9, #10, #13, and #14 (all 8 Oxford sizes); and Craftsman setting 1 (the longest loop possible with the Craftsman at 0.75"). Rug yarn, worsted-weight yarn (both Kelly's own brand: DKW yarns). Finished with a corded edge made with worsted-weight yarn. Kelly's pro tip: "In order to get the loops clipped evenly, I wrapped a band of paper around them, like a paper collar. The paper kept the loops upright and served as a ruler. After the clipping was done, I removed the collar and discarded it."

"With this piece I wanted to call attention to the extraordinary work of Swedish artist Hilma af Klint (1862–1944). Her work gives a sense of energy and a way of viewing the world that is emancipating."

SCULPTING

Free-Form Landscape. Advanced Oxford Certified Instructor Una Walker, La Grande, Oregon. 12" × 12". Background: Oxford fine #13 and #14, using the stem stitch. Main body: Sculpted with Oxford fine #13 and Oxford regular #8, #9, #10, and #13. Worsted-weight yarn.

"The limited color palette really exaggerates the movement in this piece. Using the stem stitch with the Oxford fine needles also helps your eyes focus on the moving parts." Learn to create the stem stitch in Amy Oxford's companion book *Punch Needle Rug Hooking: Your Complete Resource to Learn & Love the Craft* (page 24).

Loki's Adventures. Advanced Oxford Certified Certified Instructor Simone Vojvodin, Dutton, Ontario, Canada. 12" × 21". Oxford regular #8, #9, and #10 and Oxford fine #8, #9, #10, and #13, with heavy and fine wool yarn. Some three-dimensional areas left unclipped and others clipped and sculpted. Background: a dark, variegated fine wool yarn with an Oxford fine #14 "in a higgledy-piggledy fashion to echo the deep darkness of the woods to help the other elements come forward." Additional technique used: fine shading. All yarns hand-dyed by Simone.

"Loki is my daughter's cat, who spends hours off in the thick of the woods. I'm certain she has grand adventures. I wanted to create a rug with a storybook-coming-to-life feel to it; I also wanted to design a rug that would showcase the effect that can be achieved using all the punch needles and various sculpting techniques."

SCULPTING 97

Look Way Up. Advanced Oxford Certified Instructor Carol Gaylor, Lindsay, Ontario, Canada. 18" × 20". Oxford regular #10 and Oxford fine #8, #9, and #10. Bulky and fine wool yarn.

"I have always been fascinated by the grace and flow of this long-necked beauty! What better way to feature him than with sculpting technique, which I learned in a class taught by Advanced Oxford Certified Instructor Simone Vojvodin."

Owl in the Bush. Advanced Oxford Certified Instructor Ingrid Hieronimus, Petersburg, Ontario, Canada. 13" × 13". **Owl:** Oxford fine #8 and 3-ply wool worsted-weight yarn; **leaves:** Oxford fine #10 and regular #10 with 3-ply wool worsted-weight yarn and some novelty yarn.

"This piece was done in a punch class to learn sculpting with yarn. The class was taught by Advanced Oxford Certified Instructor Simone Vojvodin."

4
Shading

Text and project design by Louise Kulp | Demo leaves punched by Amy Oxford

THE SHADED LEAVES PROJECT

Louise Kulp. Shaded Leaves Project. Dia. 8.75". Wool on cotton.

This chapter teaches two shading techniques in one project. The first technique is called "mock shading" (*bottom leaf*), and the second is called "fingering" (*top leaf*).

Pattern size: 8" diameter

You will need:

- Monk's cloth size: 20" × 20" or size needed to fit your frame
- 14" × 14" Oxford Gripper Strip Lap Frame
- Oxford Punch Needle regular #10
- Small, sharp embroidery scissors
- Bent-handled scissors
- Mark-B-Gone or other water-soluble pen
- Sweater depiller (optional)

Yarn needed:

- 100% wool rug-weight ("bulky") yarn as shown in the step-by-step photos
- Background: Violet Jane Caribbean Sands and Desert Sands, total 1.8 ounces. Leaves: Judith Hotchkiss Design and Dyeworks Teal values 1–5 and Spearmint values 2–6. Border: Seal Harbor Rug Company SR8 (red) and SY8 (gold). Leaf veins: Several yards of color(s) complementary to your leaves. Because you need only a small amount, poke around in your yarn stash to see what you already have. I used medium pink and light pink.

- Yellow Green (fingered leaf)
  3 yards for each value:

  Value 1 (lightest)

  Value 2

  Value 3

  Value 4

  Value 5 (darkest)

- Blue Green (mock shaded leaf)
  3 yards for each value:

  Value 1 (lightest)

  Value 2

  Value 3

  Value 4

  Value 5 (darkest)

TOTAL YARN: 4 ounces

The pattern is available as a download at www.schiffercraft.com/intermediate&advancedpunchneedle.

In a Nutshell

- **Shading** in rug hooking refers to using **multiple values** of **one color** to create realistic effects. Think of color as an umbrella term with value as one of its elements. **Blue** is a color and **Light Blue** is a value.

- Why is shading (often called "multivalue shading") considered an advanced technique? It requires a trained eye in order to analyze an object and break it down into values. It also requires the artist to follow the contour of an object (directional hooking) while simultaneously laying in values. For example, if I want to hook an apple using five values of red, I follow its round shape as I fill it in with values.

THE LEGACY OF SHADING

Shading has long been the purview of traditional rug hookers. (To keep terminology simple, we will use the words "traditional rug hooking" to refer to the technique of pulling loops of wool fabric strips up through rug backing, using a tool with a hook.) Its roots in that craft lie so deep that it is almost impossible to begin a discussion of shading with a punch needle without first putting it into a traditional context. This is especially true of *fine shading*, where thin wool strips of eight (or more!) values of the same color—from very light to very dark—are used to hook realistic flowers, leaves, fruits, and scrolls. One rose petal may contain all eight values, blended with expertise by the rug-hooking artist. To fit all of those values into one petal, obviously the wool strips cannot be very wide. It is common practice to use an eight-value swatch in 3-cut wool strips (3/32" wide). The completed rose will look so real you'd be tempted to pick it right off the rug!

Take some time to research Pearl McGown, Joan Moshimer, Jane Olson, and Jeanne Field, and you will see *many* examples of exquisite rugs made by these fiber artists and their students. All four women were fine shading pioneers as well as teachers and successful entrepreneurs. Except for McGown, they were contemporaries, having been born in the 1920s (McGown was born in 1891).

BIBLIOGRAPHY

Field, Jeanne. *Shading Flowers: The Complete Guide for Rug Hookers*. Mechanicsburg, PA: Stackpole Books, 1991.

Green, Jane Halliwell. *Rugs in Bloom: Shading Flowers in Hooked Rugs*. Mechanicsburg, PA: Stackpole Books, 2012.

Moshimer, Joan. *The Complete Book of Rug Hooking*. New York: Dover, 1989.

Shepherd, Gene, ed. *The Rug Hooker's Bible: The Best from 30 Years of Jane Olson's Rugger's Roundtable*. Lemoyne, PA: Stackpole Books, 2005.

SHADING IN PUNCH NEEDLE RUG HOOKING

If traditional rug hooking is the mother of fine shading, then punch needle is certainly an offspring. Many aspects of punch needle rug hooking and traditional rug hooking are analogous: worsted-weight yarn is comparable to 3-cut strips, and rug yarn is comparable to 8-cut strips (¼" wide). Monk's cloth works well as a backing for both. Most dye formulas and methods are as applicable to dyeing yarn as they are to dyeing yardage. Five or six values of either material are enough to effectively shade larger shapes, using rug yarn or wide-cut strips. The resulting style tends to be primitive or stylized. Eight values work well for fine shading, using worsted-weight wool or 3-cut strips. The resulting style tends to be refined and realistic. The respective tools used to make loops must be appropriate to the scale of the materials. And the variety of shading techniques originally developed for traditional rug hooking can be applied equally successfully for punch needle rug hooking.

Traditional rug hookers use *swatches* to make shaded rugs. One might say, for example, "I need a periwinkle swatch for my pansy." For the longest time I didn't know what they were talking about! I mean, aren't swatches those squares of upholstery fabric hanging along the wall of a furniture store? Or those little paper strips of paint colors? In traditional rug hooking, a swatch is a group of wool fabric pieces of the *same color* but *different values*. Eight is a common number of values in fine shading. Each value is identified by a number, with 1

Top: Five values of green rug yarn. Each skein is one ounce.
Bottom: Five values of green wool yardage.

the lightest and 8 the darkest. There are five- and six-value swatches for larger cuts, and even 12- and 16-value swatches for extremely detailed work. I liken hooking with the latter to an extreme sport that should be in the Olympics!

All of this swatch talk translated into Punch Needle Speak means that we shade with multiple values of either worsted-weight yarn in an Oxford fine point needle or rug yarn in a regular point needle. And instead of a strip of wool yardage per value, we'll use a small skein of yarn per value.

Mushroom Bell Pull in progress, shown with five values of fine-cut mushroom-colored wool. Designed by Pearl McGown and Jane McGown Flynn, hooked by Louise Kulp.

Jacobean Floral. Amy Oxford, Cornwall, Vermont. 17" × 15". Oxford fine #14 and worsted-weight wool yarn. Amy adapted this pattern from a quilt design by Patricia B. Campbell, as featured in her book *The Best of Jacobean Applique*. The flowers and stems are done with mock shading, and the leaves are done with fingering. Amy used eight values of blue and eight values of green.

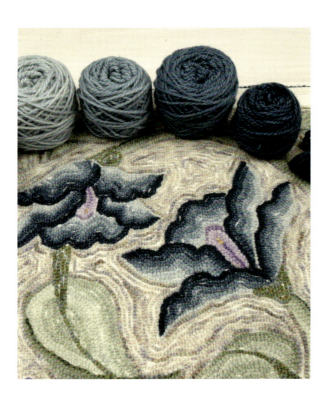

WORDS ABOUT DYEING

Where does one acquire yarn in all of these beautiful colors and values?

Excellent question! A simple Google search for "rug hooking yarn" is a good, basic place to start. Look for suppliers that offer a wide range of colors, and especially for those that offer colors cards with actual yarn samples. Yarn color cards can be a bit pricey because they are labor intensive to make, but they're a worthwhile investment and may save you money in the long run.

Look for yarn sellers in the advertisements in *Rug Hooking* magazine. And while you're there, read the articles about dyeing and color. Traditional rug hooking and punch needle rug hooking have many things in common, and dyeing wool is one of them.

Ask your fiber artist friends, fellow guild members, and workshop classmates where they get their yarn, if they dye their own yarn, if they'll dye *your* own yarn, or, better yet, if they'll teach you how! Most of us who have been practicing this craft for a while have a network of fellow rug makers who collectively possess a wealth of experience and knowledge.

If you already dye some of your own solid-color yarn, take the leap into value dyeing. The leap is small and very rewarding.

There's an excellent book by Ingrid Hieronimus called *Primary Fusion* (Ontario, Canada: Ragg Thyme Studio) that teaches an easy method for value dyeing. She uses eight canning jars in a large roasting pan on the stove, putting increasing amounts of dye in each jar to create the different values. You need only four PRO Chemical acid dyes—three primary colors and black—to make every color in the rainbow. Ingrid's book includes 58 formulas.

SHADING TECHNIQUES

The various shading techniques range in skill level from easy to advanced and include primitive, mock shading, fingering, feathering, and probably more (like the one you will invent yourself!). The Shaded Leaves Project in this chapter uses two of the most common: mock shading and fingering.

All the methods have one thing in common: the number of values of one color that can be shaded successfully must correspond to (1) the size of the space you need to fill and (2) the thickness of the yarn you're using to fill it. (Punch needle point size matters too, but we already know to use an Oxford regular point needle with rug yarn and a fine point with worsted-weight yarn.)

Here's a good example: These tiny leaves from *Bee Skep* (below) are punched with rug yarn. I had on hand seven values of a beautiful green that I wanted to use for the leaves. There was no way I could fit all seven values into those small shapes, so I chose three and still managed to shade each leaf by fingering.

Bee Skep, detail of fingered leaves. I skipped values 1, 3, 5, and 7 and used 2, 4, and 6. Skipping values results in a leaf with more contrast. Use three consecutive values if you want subtler shading.

I used mock shading for a second set of leaves, again choosing only three of the seven values.

BEGINNING THE PROJECT

Shaded Leaves is 8" in diameter and uses rug-weight yarn, an Oxford regular #10, and five values each of two leafy greens. The leaves are identical in shape, but one is made with mock shading and the other uses fingering (figure 1). Simply changing the technique results in two very different-looking leaves. Shading has so much potential to add interest to our rugs!

The bottom leaf employs *mock shading*. Its vein serves as a horizontal dividing line. Each half of the leaf has a different sequence of values moving away from the vein (light to dark and dark to light). The values are placed next to each other in rows.

The top leaf uses *fingering*. It has a more natural appearance because the values "overlap," like feathers on a bird. This leaf is shaded from stem to tip, respectively dark to light. The vein does not serve as a dividing line because the shading above and below the vein is identical.

And don't forget! As you are managing all of this placement of values, you are also using directional hooking to maintain the shape's contour.

DIAGRAMS AND DRAWINGS

I've yet to see a rug-hooking book or class handout in which shading instructions weren't accompanied by a diagram showing where to place the values. Diagrams serve as maps to guide the reader or student in the placement of values within a design element. The word "guide" is important! It is up to the rug hooker to refer back and forth between their rug pattern and the shading diagram and interpret as they see fit.

There are many styles of shading diagrams. The diagrams we created for the Shaded Leaves Project are typical of the ones used by many rug-hooking teachers. (Drawings and diagrams by Louise Kulp and Cotey Gallagher.)

Pencil-shaded rendition of mock shaded leaf

A useful exercise for any rug hooker embarking on a new shading project is drawing a pencil-shaded rendition of the motif they're going to make. This is a practice born of traditional rug hooking. It helps the maker visualize what the finished motif will look like, and, more importantly, understand the pacing of the values in relation to the space they need to fill. I like to make my value drawings on tracing paper so I can trace the outline of my motif before I color it in. My favorite tool is a set of colored pencils that range in value from "barely there" gray to "nearly black" charcoal. A regular #2 pencil and a piece of photocopier paper will work just as well. Use what you have!

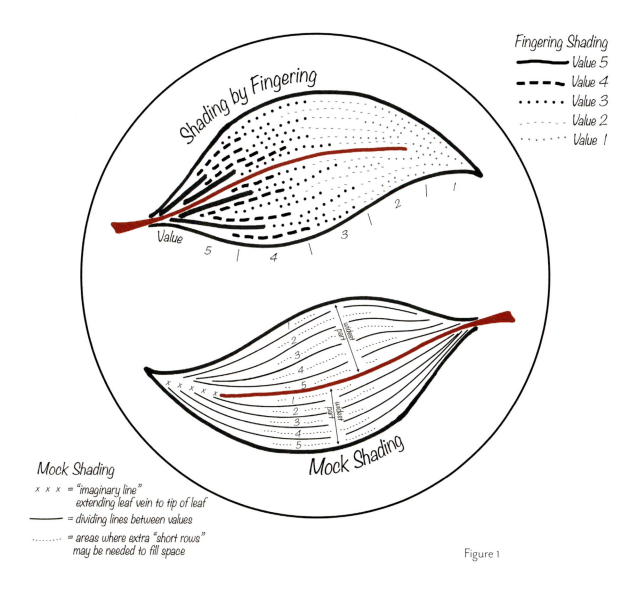

Figure 1

MOCK SHADED LEAF

Mock shading is a great place to start our shading journey because it is a straightforward method, easy to understand and to work. It also is the less intricate of the two techniques used in our project. My teacher Peggy Hannum used to say, "Let the values do all the work," and I would reply, "That's fine with me!" This is especially true in mock shading, which is as simple as placing the values of a single color next to each other in order from dark to light or light to dark. Within this simple construct are a myriad of ways to accomplish it. Our project leaf shades from dark to light from the vein to the outer edge on one half, and from light to dark from the vein to the outer edge on the other half. Other artists might choose to shade from light to dark out from the vein on both sides, or vice versa. Try making pencil-shaded drawings of the variations and choose the one you like best.

Mock shaded leaf (back)

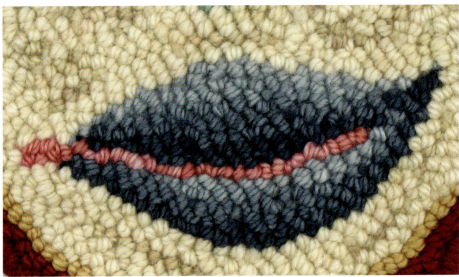

Mock shaded leaf (front)

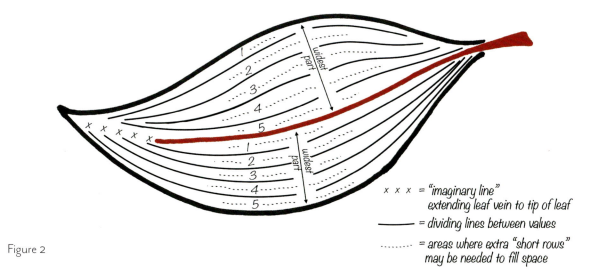

Figure 2

My leaf is a rich blue green that I dyed in eight values. Because we're shading a relatively small motif with rug yarn, using all eight values would jam-pack the loops into too small an area. The mat would end up lumpy, and it wouldn't be pleasant to make. I used my pencil-shaded drawing (see page 110) to help me determine that five values would fill my leaf nicely. When planning you can keep in mind that a row of rug yarn is approximately ⅛" thick.

The diagram for this leaf is pretty typical of the ones you'll see in books and class handouts (figure 2). It has lines, numbers, arrows, and a few little x's. A legend explains what they mean: the numbers and solid lines show where the values go, arrows indicate the widest parts of the design where you'll have to double up on some values with shorter rows (shown by dashed lines), and the x's indicate an "invisible line" that extends from the vein out to the tip of the leaf.

Make sure to understand that the *number of lines* in a diagram doesn't necessarily correspond to the *number of rows* to punch. It is up to the maker to train their artist's eye to guide them in the distribution of every value they are using to fill a design area (figure 2).

Pro Tip: Relax your stitch size and row spacing when you shade with rug yarn. The shading you're working so diligently on will be tidier and better defined if there's a bit of breathing room between values. I make four stitches per inch and aim for about six rows per inch in the shaded parts of a rug pattern. Give your motifs crisp shapes by outlining them with one row of background punched at six stitches per inch.

SHADING 113

MAKING THE MOCK SHADED LEAF: BOTTOM HALF

Step 1. Punch the vein first to establish a dividing line between the top and bottom halves of the leaf. Use six stitches per inch for a well-defined line. All your other leaf stitches will be four stitches per inch. Remember not to overpack!

Since mock shading is a straightforward technique, you may want to "freehand" punch each value simply by referring back and forth between the diagram and your pattern. If you want to work more precisely, feel free to draw the segments right onto your pattern with a Sharpie or water-soluble pen.

Step 2. All five values converge at the stem. At the tip of the leaf, each value stops along an imaginary line that extends the vein line to the tip. This is shown on figure 2 by tiny x's. I like to make the invisible line temporarily visible by drawing it in with a water-soluble pen, such as the Mark-B-Gone.

Step 3. Punch the darkest value (value 5) along the entire outside edge, starting at the very tip of the leaf and ending at the stem. Use four stitches per inch and punch right on the line.

Step 4. Follow the value 5 row with one row each of values 4, 3, 2, and 1, in that order. Value 1 will be along the vein. Each of these rows starts at the imaginary line. When they're all in, one yarn tail of each value will span the imaginary row when seen from the front.

Step 5. At the stem, each consecutive value will end by squishing into the ever-narrowing empty space below the vein.

1

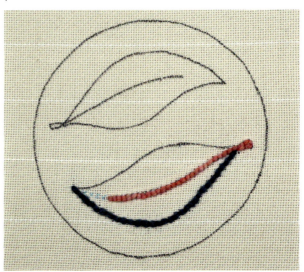

2, 3

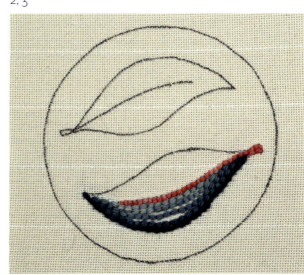

4, 5, 6

7

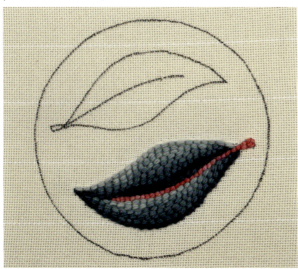

Top half of leaf completed

Step 6. You will need to fill in at the widest part of the leaf (shown on figure 2—page 113—by an arrow) with shorter rows of some of the values (shown on figure 2 by dashed lines). Here I've filled in some of the gaps, and you can see I still have some values left to fill in.

Step 7. Complete the bottom half of the leaf before you move on to the top half.

MAKING THE MOCK SHADED LEAF: TOP HALF

Proceed with the top half of the leaf with the same technique you used with the bottom, punching one value at a time.

Step 1. Punch a single row of value 1 along the entire outside edge. Start one stitch in from the tip of the leaf and end at the stem. Use four stitches per inch and punch right on the line.

Step 2. Punch a single row of value 5 along the vein (including the invisible part). Start in the same hole where you started the value 1 row you just punched, and end at the stem.

Step 3. Punch values 2, 3, and 4, distributing them evenly to fill the space. Double up on values as needed to fill in the widest part of this half.

Step 4. Remember to use directional hooking! It is a little trickier this time because you have both a "hill" contour (the outer edge) and a "dale" contour (the vein). Make sure they meet amicably in the middle!

Step 5. Clip and poke all the ends on the front side of the leaf. Since you worked so carefully to lay in your values, take the time to poke the loops into place according to value.

FINGERED LEAF

Fingering differs from mock shading because the values blend *into* each other instead of lying *beside* each other. It produces a more natural look. The values are placed something like this: short rows of value 4 emerge from between short rows of value 5, short rows of value 3 emerge from between short rows of value 4, and so on. Punching starts at the stem with value 5. The values will fan out until we reach the widest part of the leaf, then taper in until we end at the tip with value 1. There is a lot of starting and stopping with this method because the rows are quite short.

Our leaf uses five values of a fresh yellow green. A vein (punch this first with six stitches per inch) bisects the leaf the same way the vein in the mock shaded leaf did, but this time it does not function as a horizontal dividing line between two different value sequences.

Fingering is a relatively complex shading technique. It requires lots of practice and some trial and error to place the values "just so." It also requires a trained eye, but the more you do it, the

Figure 3. The pencil-shaded drawing will help you envision how your completed leaf will look.

better trained your eye will become. Fingering is a very rewarding technique to learn and use because the results are so lovely. Your friends will take one look at your rug and exclaim, "How did you make that leaf (rose petal, bunch of grapes, butterfly wing, etc.) look so real?" That reaction alone is worth learning how to finger!

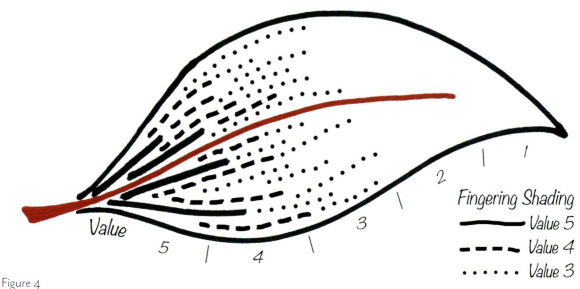

Figure 4

The shading technique "fingering" takes its name from the way our fingers interlace when we wedge our left-hand fingers in between our right-hand fingers. We want our values to do the same thing.

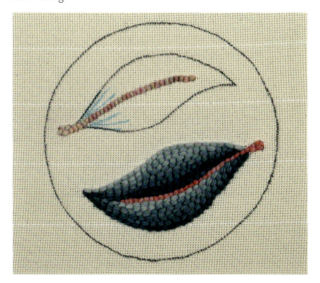

1

2

You will see that the fingering diagram (figure 4) has guide lines only for values 5 (solid), 4 (dashed), and 3 (dotted). Values 2 and 1 are left to your trained eye. By the time you're ready for value 2, you'll have a pretty good idea of the way the values need to merge. Keep in mind that the lines are *guides only* to help you get started. They are not exact representations of the rows you'll punch.

The diagram includes additional marks across the bottom of the leaf just outside the outline. They slice the leaf vertically into five more or less equal segments. These segments indicate where the corresponding value will be concentrated. For example, value 3 is concentrated in the segment marked "3." Some of value 3 will dip down into segment 4 and extend up into segment 2.

MAKING THE FINGERED LEAF

1. First punch the vein at six stitches per inch. Punch everything else with four stitches per inch, and don't crowd the loops or your leaf will be as puffy as a little leaf pillow! Notice that the fingers radiating out from the base of the leaf are few and short. Refer to the diagram to guide you in their placement and length. I like to draw them in freehand with a Mark-B-Gone pen for a little extra security. These fingers lay the foundation for all the fingers that follow.

2. Start your shading at the base of the leaf with a few fingers in value 5 (the darkest). I find that I get better results when I punch *toward* the stem. Try for yourself punching toward the stem and away from it. One direction might suit you better than the other. This is the only value 5 in the entire leaf.

3. Start fingering with value 4. Place the rows/fingers of value 4 *in between* the rows of value 5, extending them a bit farther out toward the widest part of the leaf. Refer to the segments marked on the diagram to help you determine where this value should be concentrated.

4. Add values 3 and 2, all the while following the contour of the leaf. You can see that we have passed the widest part of the leaf and are tapering toward the tip. Only value 1 (the lightest) is left to fill in.

5. Fill in value 1. Emphasize the point by using the following pro tip.

3

4

***Pro Tip:* Making a point** The graceful contour of our leaf has a pointy V-shaped tip. Emphasize the point by working out to the very tip on the longest side of the leaf (the top), then cut the yarn and poke the end through to the front. Start the other side of the "V" one stitch in from the tip.

5

6

6. My leaf is finished, but the front is a mess! I can't even tell how my fingering looks. Instead of clipping away at my yarn tails—because I'm so eager to see my beautiful shading—I'll exercise patience and evaluate the shading from the back, making any necessary final adjustments before I clip. Don't hesitate to pull out rows that don't meet your expectations and try them again.

7. Now at long last it's time to clip the front. It's tempting to hold multiple ends and cut them all at once, but resist this urge and cut them one at a time. Bent-handled scissors work beautifully for this task. Make sure to cut the ends flush with the loops. You might find that some ends become one value darker after clipping, and that even though you've cut them flush, they are still a bit fuzzy. This is the time to pull out your trusty sweater depiller! Use it on the front of your work while pushing down gently in small circular motions. Those fuzzy ends will disappear, creating a crisp, professional look.

CONTRAST

Our fingered leaf is finished, and we've even punched the background and border. Isn't all of this fabulous? But . . . upon further review it looks to me like the stem fades into the background, and so does the tip of the leaf. They don't show up very well against the background. There isn't enough *contrast*.

I mentioned above that my traditional rug-hooking teacher, Peggy, advised her students to let the values do all the work. She also said, "Contrast is king!" Shading isn't just about value; it's also about contrast. While the subtle differences between values make our designs look natural, it is the contrast between background and motif that makes the latter the star.

Correcting contrast is easy in punch needle rug hooking. We'll fix the stem first. The stem (and vein) yarn is mostly light pink, with occasional darker spots. Unfortunately, when I was making

SHADING   119

the leaf the dark spots didn't fall at the stem. I wish they had—the stem would have shown up a lot better against the light background (a spot-dyed yarn called "parchment").

I cut a segment of stem yarn at its very darkest part and repunched the stem with it. I didn't need much—the stem portion of the vein is only eight loops.

I used two tricks at the tip of the leaf to increase its contrast against the background. First, I pulled out the two short rows of value 1 that outlined the tip, and replaced them with value 2. Next, I cut a segment of parchment at its darkest part and repunched the background around the tip with it.

Pro Tip: Monk's cloth is woven with double horizontal and vertical threads that make up a grid of tiny squares. The grid makes it easy to punch straight lines, but when your lines curve, you have to make adjustments. To make curves as smooth as possible, punch some of your stitches *in between* the double threads of a square.

FINAL WORDS OF ADVICE

Evaluate your work in progress often. View it from across the room and trust your eyes to tell you if the shading needs adjustment. Evaluate it from the back (wrong side); the front will be too messy.

Don't be too hard on yourself if your first attempt at fingering doesn't look as good as you think it should. Mastery of fingering comes with practice!

Amy's completed Shaded Leaves Project. Oxford Certified Instructor Cotey Gallagher did a beautiful job with the whip stitching!

A Note from Amy

WHAT I LEARNED FROM MAKING LOUISE'S SHADED LEAVES PROJECT

- This piece is a wonderful jumping-off point—with these techniques you can shade anything!
- I learned a new way to make a point (see Louise's pro tip on page 118). To get a sharp point on a leaf, star, or other pointy object, I have always punched one stitch past the point, cut and ended, and then picked up again going down the other side of the point by ducking in along the side of the last stitch. Louise does it a bit differently and still gets a beautiful point. I like her way just as much.

ADDING SHADING TO YOUR WORK—ENCOURAGEMENT FROM AMY

As beginning punchers, most of us learned to fill in areas with what I call "outline and fill." This is just what it sounds like, outlining an area and then filling it in, usually following the shape of the object. As a teacher, I like to give my students a challenge when I know they're ready to take the next step. My guess is that if you've made it this far, you're ready for a challenge too!

My suggested challenge is to add some shading to your next project. It doesn't have to be anything as intricate as using six shades for fingering or mock shading. You can add depth and a new level of interest and beauty to your work by just adding one or two more values to that orange—a highlight in a lighter value and a shadow along one side, for example. Think about where the light source is coming from to decide what area will be lighter and what will be in shadow. Shading isn't just for leaves, flowers, and fruit! Try looking at your design with shading in mind, and think about where you can add more values.

How many times have you found yourself going around and around, filling in a special and important element in your rug, feeling bored? (When will this rooster ever *end*?!) This is a perfect time to add more values here and there. I always say that if a rug is boring to punch, it might be boring to look at!

Shading Certification Samples. Advanced Oxford Certified Instructor Louise Kulp, Lancaster, Pennsylvania. Each mat is 15" × 15".

"The design is adapted from a 6" × 6" blue and white earthenware tile manufactured by Maw & Co. / Benthall Works, Jackfield, Shropshire, England (probably early 20th century). Compare sample 1 (*above*) and sample 2 (*right*)."

- Light background vs. dark background
- Design for 3-ply rug yarn in regular point needle vs. design for worsted-weight yarn in fine point needle
- The same design in two colorways
- Mock shading and fingering vs. a more stylized approach (placing colors "by eye" and using variegated yarn to add interest)

Sample 1: Oxford regular #10 and 3-ply wool rug yarn. Mock shading and fingering shading, each done with six values.

Sample 2: Oxford fine #13 and #14 and worsted-weight wool yarn. Using two needle sizes to render a design in relief. The objects (flowers and leaves) are made with the Oxford fine #13, so they stand out in relief against the lower background loops punched with the Oxford fine #14. The center lines in the borders that divide the quadrants also recede.

Lupines with Fine Yarn. Advanced Oxford Certified Instructor Judith Hotchkiss, Deer Isle, Maine. 14" diameter. Oxford fine #14 with worsted-weight wool yarn.

Lupines with Bulky Yarn. Advanced Oxford Certified Instructor Judith Hotchkiss, Deer Isle, Maine. 14" diameter. Oxford regular #9 with 3-ply wool rug yarn.

"Lupines are one of my favorite flowers, and I wanted to show the difference between a pattern shaded with fine yarn versus one shaded with rug yarn. I was able to use six values with thinner yarn but had room for only three values with bulky yarn. Note that both pieces use variegated yarn for the flowers and leaves, shaking up the traditional shaded look."

Spring Flowers. Oxford Certified Instructor Cilla Cameron, Nottingham, United Kingdom. 15" × 24".

"Inspiration came from a paper collage I made. I cut the template for the flowers from the collage. The flowers and vase were punched with an Oxford fine #10, and the background with an Oxford fine #14. The flowers stand out slightly from the background, giving a 3-D effect."

Leaves—a Study in Shading. Advanced Oxford Certified Instructor Heidi Whipple, Cornwall, Vermont. 13" × 13". *Clockwise starting at upper left*: 1. No shading with outline and fill. 2. Fingering shading with rug yarn and an Oxford regular #10. 3. Light side / dark side. 4. Fingering shading with worsted-weight yarn and an Oxford fine #14. The background is an example of mock shading for an ombré effect.

Tiger Lilies. Advanced Oxford Certified Instructor Kim Scanlan, St. Paul, Minnesota. 12" × 12". Oxford fine #13 and #14, wool worsted-weight yarn.

"Tiger lilies are a great inspiration for a sampler on shading! I had to repunch some areas a few times to get the petals to lie correctly. I hand-dyed all the yarn for the lilies and stems."

Floating World. Advanced Oxford Certified Instructor Kelly Wright, Icking, Bavaria, Germany. 12" × 12". Oxford regular #9 and D. K. Wright rug yarn.

"An approach to fine shading. Flowers, berries, a banner, and a fairy in a bubble are part of my piece *Ukiyo*, an unusual interpretation for the Japanese term referring to an art movement but meaning 'Floating World.'"

Strawberry Patch Friends. Oxford Certified Instructor Heidi J. Martin, Melbourne, Florida. 33" × 20". Animals, berries, and leaves shaded with 2-ply wool yarn in eight values each for the rabbit, fox, bird, strawberries, and leaves. Strawberry seeds are Czechoslovakian glass seed beads, sewn into the yarn loops with needle and thread.

"This was designed after a day of picking berries near my house. I encountered a lot of wildlife and decided to capture the relationship among the animals who resided there. Wanting to create a realistic animal figure, I decided to employ multiple values of a color and use the shading technique with this rug. Steaming was important to do before adding the embellishment beads."

Disillusionment. Oxford Certified Instructor Heidi J. Martin, Melbourne, Florida. 46" × 34". The face is shaded using seven values of black single-ply wool yarn and an Oxford fine #13. The rest of the piece is value-on-value shading, using eight values of red and three values of green, 3-ply wool yarn, and an Oxford regular #11.

"This rug showcases fine shading techniques used in the face (fingering shading) and value on value throughout the rest (mock shading). Using the same color (red), dark values placed on light values reverse as the piece progresses to the right, ending up with light on dark. The rug symbolizes the artist's contained frustration."

Purple Anemone Wildflower. Advanced Oxford Certified Instructor Cotey Gallagher, Salisbury, Vermont. 15" × 26". **Flowers and leaves:** fine shading (fingering) with wool rug-weight and worsted-weight yarn and an Oxford fine #10; **background:** punched by alternating rows of two yarn colors with an Oxford regular #10.

"This is the first of an A-to-Z series of floral rugs I am adapting from my original series of Art Nouveau–inspired paintings."

Grami's Hibiscus. Alaina Dickason Roberts, Underhill, Vermont. 24" × 36". **Hibiscus flower and leaves:** Oxford fine #10 and worsted-weight yarn from Judith Hotchkiss Design and Dyeworks. The hibiscus features 19 colors in a variety of values, and the leaves have eight values. **Border and vines:** Oxford regular #10 and 8-cut wool fabric strips. **Background:** Assorted Oxford Punch Needle sizes with 3-ply wool rug yarn.

"This rug was inspired by my great-grandmother's prolific flower garden in St. Thomas, United States Virgin Islands, from which she would pick hibiscus daily."

5
Punching with Fabric Strips

Text and project design by Louise Kulp | Demo project punched by Heidi Whipple

THE FLOWER PROJECT

Louise Kulp. Flower Project. 9" × 7". Wool on cotton.

Pattern size: 9" high × 7" wide

You will need:

- Monk's cloth size: 20" × 20" or size needed to fit your frame
- 14" × 14" Oxford Gripper Strip Lap Frame
- Oxford regular point punch needle size #10
- Oxford fine point punch needles sizes #10 and #14 (optional)
- Fabric strip cutter OR rotary cutter and cutting mat
- No. 6 cutter head. If you don't have a 6, you can use a #7 or #8.
- No. 3 cutter head (optional)
- A kitchen "scrubby" made of netting

"Yarn" needed:

- 100% wool fabric as listed on page 142

For more about punching with fabric strips, please see Amy Oxford's companion book *Punch Needle Rug Hooking: Your Complete Resource to Learn & Love the Craft* (pages 180–185).

In a Nutshell

- The same wool fabric strips that traditional rug hookers use to make loops can be used in a punch needle.
- The *cut* (or width) of the strip is matched to the size of punch needle it works best with.
- A narrow strip of fabric makes different-looking loops than a strand of yarn does, because yarn is round and fabric is flat. This difference is compensated for by adjusting punching technique.
- Punching with wool strips is considerably faster than traditional hooking with wool strips, because the punch needle does a lot of the work for you.

It's common to think of fabric strips as a material exclusive to traditional rug hooking, and yarn as the material of choice for punch needle rug hooking. But did you know that fabric strips can be used with a punch needle, just as yarn can be used with a rug hook? There is even a beloved style called Chéticamp—named after its village of origin on Cape Breton Island, Nova Scotia—that uses yarn and a hook (but that's a story for another book!).

Chéticamp-style mat front. Contemporary Chéticamp mat, wool yarn on burlap, 4.5" × 4.5". Purchased at the Hooked Rug Museum of North America, Nova Scotia.

Back of Chéticamp mat

Loops are loops no matter what materials and tools are used to make them. Creative hookers of all strips(!) even combine loops of yarn and fabric in the same piece. They get the best of both worlds without having to switch tools, and the results can be spectacular.

If you've never used wool strips in a punch needle, give it a try! It's a wonderful technique to have in your repertoire and will open up an entirely new world of materials, colors, textures, and special effects that you can apply to your work. All it takes is a little practice and a few minor adjustments to the punching techniques you already know. Read on to find out what happens when a punch needle rug hooker lets loose with a piece of wool!

YARN IS ROUND, FABRIC IS FLAT

The very nature of fabric strips (they're flat) requires punch needle rug hookers to make some simple adjustments to familiar techniques. Tweak a process here and a motion there, and you'll be enamored with wool strips in no time.

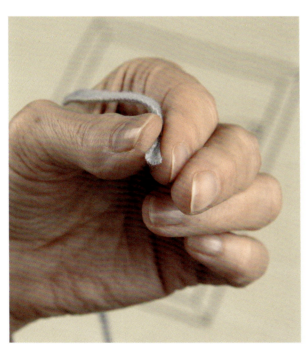

Threading a punch needle. Fold the very tip of your wool strip in half, forming a V shape. Thread this pinched end through the eye of the needle.

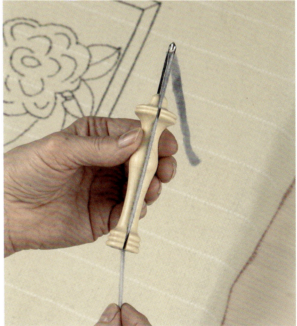

Slip the other end of the strip into the slot (a perfect fit!), and tug as usual until the strip disappears into the needle channel.

PUNCHING WITH FABRIC STRIPS

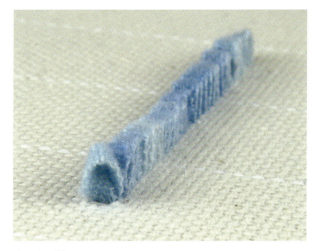

A twisted loop

Untwisting a twist. Unlike a strand of yarn, a fabric strip has two distinct sides and can twist along its length, causing lumps and bumps. Most twists smooth out as the strip travels through the needle channel. If one does find its way into your rug, simply pull out the offending loop, undo the twist, and remake the stitch.

Punching curves. We already know to punch with the open side of the needle channel facing the direction we're going. After a while we don't even think about it, as automatic as this action becomes. When you punch a curved line with a fabric strip, however, needle direction needs to be more deliberate. You must turn the punch needle in tiny increments—sometimes with every stitch—in order to get a graceful line. Fortunately, the Flower Project in this chapter has lots of curves, so you'll get plenty of practice!

STRIP WIDTHS AND PUNCH NEEDLE SIZES

STRIP WIDTH DEMYSTIFIED

The width of a strip of wool for rug hooking is measured in 32nds of an inch. For example, a 6-cut strip is $6/32"$ wide. Many traditional rug hookers purchase fabric-cutting machines and individual (interchangeable) blades or cutter heads to go in them. Cutter heads can range in size from 2 to 10; the 3 to 8 range is most popular. Using narrower cuts such as 3 and 4 often is referred to as fine hooking. Using wider cuts such as 7 and 8 is called primitive hooking. Falling somewhere in between are 5- and 6-cuts. The Flower Project in this chapter uses 6-cut strips with some 3-cut for detail and dimension.

GUIDELINES FOR MATCHING PUNCH NEEDLE SIZE WITH STRIP WIDTH

3-CUT STRIPS (3/32")

Use an Oxford fine #14.

Punch into every single hole of the monk's cloth (12 stitches per inch).

Leave either one row or no row of empty holes between punched rows, depending on wool fabric weight.

4-CUT STRIPS (4/32", A.K.A. 1/8")

Use an Oxford fine #13 or #14.

Punch into two consecutive holes, then skip a hole; repeat. In other words, punch-punch-skip (eight stitches per inch).

Alternate between one row of empty holes / no row of empty holes between punched rows.

6-CUT STRIPS (6/32")

Use an Oxford regular #10.

Punch into every other hole of the monk's cloth (six stitches per inch).

Leave one row of empty holes between punched rows.

7-CUT STRIPS (7/32") AND 8-CUT STRIPS (8/32" A.K.A. 1/4")

Use an Oxford regular #10.

Punch into every other hole of the monk's cloth (six stitches per inch).

Leave two rows of empty holes between punched rows.

SHOULD YOU PURCHASE A FABRIC CUTTER?

A good fabric cutter is an investment. If you don't already own one, it's best to ask a rug-hooking friend to cut some strips for you to try out with your punch needle. If you like the technique and know you'll do more of it, then it makes sense to consider buying your own cutter.

Alternatively, you can ask the vendor you buy wool from if they'll cut the strips for you in the size you need. Usually there is a small surcharge for this service. You also can cut wool into strips by hand, either with a ruler and rotary cutter or by "eyeballing" the width and cutting with scissors. Wide strips are easier to cut than narrow ones; less dangerous, too, if you're using a rotary cutter. To put this in perspective, remember that rug hookers of old cut *all* of their strips with scissors!

Fabric woven with complex weave structures such as twills, tweeds, and herringbone tends to fray when feeding through the punch needle, but plain weaves work beautifully. That being said, you never know unless you test a fabric. Plain weaves also tend to wear better than complex weaves.

Traditional rug hookers use a rule of thumb for loop height: pull a loop as high as the strip is wide. In other words, an 8-cut (¼" wide) strip is pulled ¼" high. Most of the punch needle size / strip width combinations in the guidelines on the previous page approximate this rule, and some are exact matches; for example, an Oxford regular #10, which makes a ¼" high loop paired with an 8-cut strip.

The loop-height "rule," like most others, can—and should!—be broken. Think instead about how you want to represent the elements in your design. Try out different needle size and strip width pairings until you find the ones that will make the rug you see in your mind's eye. In the Flower Project, I used 6- and 3-cut strips and both regular and fine point needles.

CHOOSING WOOL

In addition to strip width, the *weight* of the wool you choose to use will guide your choice of punch needle size. Wool fabric is woven in a range of weights from heavy to light. Compare the hand, or feel, of a winter blazer with that of a summer wrap. In the "wrong" size of needle, a heavy or densely woven wool will drag through the needle channel; a light or loosely woven strip will slip out. Either way, loops will not form properly in the monk's cloth. Wool can also fray or shred if it is lightweight and cut too fine. If you can hold a piece of wool up to the light and see through it, it's probably too thin to punch with.

Some wool is too loosely woven to hold together in 3-cut strip but holds together well in 4-cut, even though the 4-cut is just a mere ¹⁄₃₂" wider!

PREPARING YOUR WOOL

Generally, 100% wool yardage needs to be machine-washed and dried before it is cut into strips for rug making. If you go "thrifting" for wool, give your purchase a hot machine wash and dry as soon as you get it home. This process felts the fibers, which makes the wool easier to cut into strips and hold together better when hooked.

Some rug-hooking shops give you the option of buying a piece of yardage washed or unwashed. Ask if you're not sure what you are buying. If you purchase hand-dyed wool from a shop or independent dyer, it already has been washed as part of the dyeing process.

HOW DO I KNOW IF IT'S 100% WOOL, SYNTHETIC, OR A WOOL/SYNTHETIC BLEND?

Cut a narrow strip and carefully hold a match to the end. If it smells like burning hair, it's wool. If it sizzles and forms a little ball, it's synthetic.

USING 4-CUT STRIPS

Many traditional rug hookers love 4-cut wool for its versatility. It holds together better than some 3-cuts and provides more detail than 6 and higher. It is an "in-between" size for punching with, though—a tad wide for a fine point Oxford punch and a tad narrow for a regular point. You may want to try 4-cut strips in a Craftsman punch needle if you have one. A Craftsman set at 10 makes the same loops as an Oxford regular #10, but its threading mechanism is such that it provides slightly more traction for the strip.

It's often said that "rug hooking is like painting with wool." The beautiful hand-dyed wools available to rug hookers today make this statement even truer. The Flower Project in this chapter *is* a painting—a still life of a brilliant red flower in a blue pottery vase, soaking up the sun in a farmhouse kitchen in Tuscany.

The Flower Project is 9" high by 7" wide. The original mat was made primarily with 6-cut wool and an Oxford regular #10; 3-cut wool and Oxford fine #13 and #14 were used as well to add some detail and dimension. It would look just as pretty punched with 6-cut strips and an Oxford regular #10 throughout. Punching the flower by itself with a complementary color background would make a small and lovely 5" square mug rug while giving you a solid introduction to punching with strips.

Oxford Punch Needles. *Left to right*: #10 regular point, #10 fine point, #14 fine point

Our project as photographed uses the following wool hand-dyed by color expert Nancy Jewett (Fluff & Peachy Bean Designs). Wool measurements are approximate. Feel free to choose your own colors and/or use what you already have.

MATERIALS NEEDED

FLOWER

Fireball, (1) 4" × 32" piece

Naked Nonpareils, (1) 4" × 16" piece **or** a small amount of any white, cream, or ivory

Light Mango Passion, (1) 4" × 16" piece **or** a small amount of a similar bright yellow orange

LEAVES

Blooming Oak Leaf, (1) 4" × 16" piece

Olive Elf, (1) 4" × 16" piece

Light Mango Passion

VASE

Great Blue Heron, values 3, 4, and 6 from (1) 8-value swatch (light, medium, and dark Blue Heron)

Naked Nonpareils

TABLE

Claret Delight, (2) 4" × 16" pieces

BACKGROUND

Pastel Fireball, (1) 4" × 32" piece

FRAME

Tree of Life, (2) 4" × 16" pieces

The pattern is available as a download at www.schiffercraft.com/intermediate&advancedpunchneedle.

THE FLOWER PROJECT: PATTERN INFO

Figure 1. This map shows where to use the different punch needle and strip cut sizes.

Oxford regular #10 and 6-cut strips are used for the vase, background, border, and most of the flowers and leaves. Oxford fine #14 and 3-cut strips are used for the leaf veins. Oxford fine #10 and 3-cut strips are used for the flower center and curved petal lines.

Note that this map is backward. This is a "working version," meaning it's mirror-imaged to be a more convenient reference when you work.

The flower design is asymmetrical, so we drew it backward on monk's cloth. With the front side facing you, the single leaf will be on the right side of the picture as originally designed.

ORDER OF PUNCHING

In a pictorial design like ours, rug hookers typically punch "what's in front" first. This helps visually establish perspective and depth and gives a more thoughtful representation of the design. In our case, most of the flower is in front except for two petals that tuck behind the top of the vase. We'll punch the flower first and use *holding lines* for the two parts of the vase in front of those petals. Next is the vase, followed by the leaves, tabletop, background, and frame, in that order.

The Flower Project is punched primarily with 6-cut strips in an Oxford regular #10, but that pairing alone couldn't give the detail desired in the flower center and petal lines. 3-cut strips in an Oxford fine #10 for those areas was tried, and it worked beautifully.

Color Chart - Working Version

Figure 2. This map shows the wool fabric strip colors and where to use them. Note that this map is backward. This is a "working version," meaning it's mirror-imaged to be a more convenient reference when you work.

PUNCHING WITH FABRIC STRIPS 145

1 (back)

1 (front)

STEP 1.

Punch the flower center and petal line details. Use 3-cut strips in an Oxford fine #10. Punch into every hole in the monk's cloth (12 stitches per inch).

STEP 2.

Holding lines: Before we start punching the flower petals, we have to consider the two petals that fall partially behind the vase. Remember that we hook the foremost elements first? In this case, bits of the vase on both sides at the top are in front of those petals. We'll use some leftover yarn or strips to punch temporary holding lines. They'll preserve the contours of the vase (and thus the perception of depth) while we finish punching the "behind" petal parts. When the petals are finished, remove the holding lines and hook the vase.

STEP 3.

Fill in the rest of the flower. Use 6-cut strips in an Oxford regular #10. Punch into every other hole in the monk's cloth (six stitches per inch) and leave an empty row of holes between punched rows.

Pro Tip: When punching with strips, don't split monk's cloth threads. Punch into the "holes proper" only, up, down, left, right, or diagonally. A stitch punched diagonally is slightly longer, but the minuscule difference does not affect the finished piece. A proper hole is more accommodating to a flat strip.

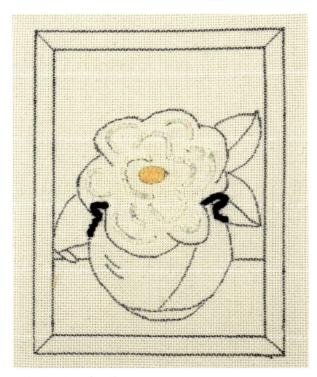
2 Holding lines (back)

2 Holding lines (front)

3 (back)

3 (front)

PUNCHING WITH FABRIC STRIPS 147

4 Veins (back)

4 Veins (front)

5 Completed leaves (back)

5 Completed leaves (front)

STEP 4.

Punch the veins in the leaves first. Use 3-cut strips in an Oxford fine #14. Punch into every hole in the monk's cloth (12 stitches per inch).

STEP 5.

Surround the veins with two colors of green as indicated in the color map (figure 2). Use 6-cut strips in an Oxford regular #10. We love the look of bright-yellow veins peeking out from the surrounding greens!

STEP 6.

Now that your flower and leaves are all filled in, you're ready to punch the vase. First pull out your holding lines. Do this from the back. These holding lines have helped us keep the lovely curves in the petals, and in the vase. Use 6-cut strips in an Oxford regular #10.

6 Remove the holding lines before you punch the vase.

Completed vase (back)

Completed vase (front)

PUNCHING WITH FABRIC STRIPS 149

7 and 8 Completed frame, table, and background (back)

7 and 8 Completed frame, table, and background (front)

9a

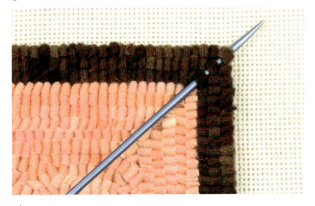

9b

STEP 7.

Punch the border, using Oxford regular #10 and 6-cut strips.

STEP 8.

Punch the table and background, using Oxford regular #10 and 6-cut strips. Fill in both with directional hooking. It is best to outline large areas such as these first and then fill them in.

STEP 9.

To get nice sharp points on the leaves, finish with a single end and clip. Use a tweezer or similar fine "pinching" tool to turn the cut end parallel to the vein (9a).

You can make the border look more like a frame by "mitering" the corners. Slide a knitting needle or other smooth thin, pointed stick through the corner stitches and position them into a diagonal line (9b). Set the line when you steam-press the mat.

FINISHING TOUCHES

Correct any too-tall or too-short loops by inserting a traditional rug hook or crochet hook into their middles and tugging gently (above left). Use a kitchen scrubby made from netting to whisk away any stray frays on the surface of your piece (above right). A scrubby is to a wool-strips rug what a depiller is to a yarn rug! Steam-press your project with the *front side facedown* on a thick terry towel to give the loops something soft to sink into.

MINIMIZING WASTE

Punching with fabric strips can waste more material than punching with yarn or traditional rug hooking with strips. It does not have to be so! We have some tricks up our sleeve to minimize waste.

When we punch with yarn, we usually are working from a continuous strand that's coming off a ball or skein. We have to end a strand and start a new one only when we change color, punch ourselves into a corner, get to the very bottom of the ball, or finish our rug.

Fabric strips, on the other hand, are very much shorter because they're cut from woven cloth. There are a lot more ends—and therefore waste—because of frequent "coming to the end of a strip and having to start a new one." Fortunately, traditional rug hookers can hook a strip to its *very end*—they have complete control because the strip passes directly through their fingers. They become very skilled at getting the most loops possible out of a treasured piece of wool.

Punchers' strips pass through a tool. There is a point toward the end of a strip when the tension on it is lost, and the last inches can't form loops that will stay in the monk's cloth. Or can they? Advanced Oxford Certified Instructor Judith Hotchkiss, our smart and talented colleague, discovered a way to punch a strip all the way to its end! When the strip stops working, she slips the final few inches out of the channel and tensions them by hand.

If you get to the end of a strip and the last few inches won't flow through the punch needle, slip the end out of the channel and punch while holding the end of the strip with slight tension.

Sometimes you have to change to another color of wool before you've used up the one that's in your punch. Don't throw away what's left of the old color, even if it looks too short to rethread. It isn't! I managed eight more loops out of the short strip shown below. Here's how I did it:

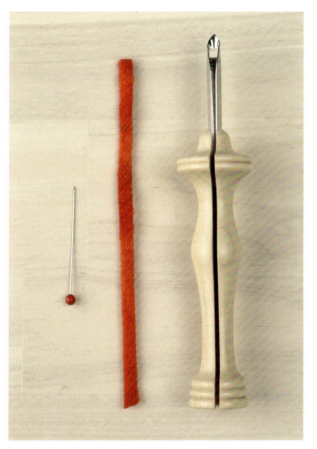

Step 1. You need a quilting pin, the strip remnant, and your punch.

Step 2. Push the remnant into the needle channel as far as it will go. **Step 3.** Use the quilting pin to lightly spear the strip in the channel. **Step 4.** Drag the strip slowly out of the channel toward the eye of the needle (shown here).
Step 5. Thread the eye of the needle.

This trick is especially good to know when you are running low on a color and need every last loop!

Fabric Strip Certification Sampler. Advanced Oxford Certified Instructor Louise Kulp, Lancaster, Pennsylvania. 15" × 15". Cardboard template traced from a flower motif in *American Hooked and Sewn Rugs: Folk Art under Foot* by Joel and Kate Kopp, with added hand-drawn leaves, 6" and 7" square cardboard templates. Oxford regular #10 with 6-cut strips; Oxford fine #14 with 3-cut strips.

The Goat at the Door. Advanced Oxford Certified Instructor Kelly Wright, Icking, Bavaria, Germany. 12" × 12". Oxford fine #14 with 3-cut wool strips. Oxford #10 regular with 6-cut and 7-cut wool strips.

"I like to use the fabric in a punch needle without trying to imitate the flow of traditional rug hooking. This piece is simply a punched illustration using a fun palette and fine-cut strips."

Fabric Strip Certification Sampler. Advanced Oxford Certified Instructor Una Walker, La Grande, Oregon. 12" × 12". Entire piece: Oxford fine #10 and Oxford regular #10 with cotton fabrics, wool strips, and repurposed T-shirt yarn. Crocheted border uses same materials, with a crochet hook size 1.

"Students often want to know, 'What can I punch with?,' and my answer is always, 'Whatever fits through the needle!' This piece also has a crocheted edge."

Lemon & Grey. Oxford Certified Instructor Cilla Cameron, Nottingham, United Kingdom. 25" × 18". Oxford regular #9 with 6-cut and 7-cut wool strips. Hand-dyed wool strips and as-is wool strips.

Fabric Strip Certification Sampler. Advanced Oxford Certified Instructor Heidi Whipple, Cornwall, Vermont. 10" × 10". **Border:** Oxford regular #10 with wool rug yarn. **Inside border:** Oxford regular #10 with 7-cut wool strips and Oxford fine #10 with 3-cut wool strips.

PUNCHING WITH FABRIC STRIPS

Teal Squared. Oxford Certified Instructor Yvonne Iten-Scott, Erin, Ontario, Canada. 28" × 17". Oxford regular #10 with 7-cut wool strips.

"This was my first geometric rug. I have always found it difficult to traditional-rug-hook in straight lines, but I did find it much easier with the punch needle. In fact, I found it quite meditative. When punching with strips it can be frustrating if the strips twist. I found if the wool was quite thin, they would twist more easily. The other thing I learned was not to pack in the strips too tightly or your lines will be wonky. You will lose the geometry of the basket weave. I tried to use each color at least twice somewhere in the rug. Although it does look like a 'hit and miss,' I did plan the colors and continued them from one end of the rug to the other."

Woollelujah. Advanced Oxford Certified Instructor Kim Scanlan, St. Paul, Minnesota. 17" × 9".

"This term perfectly captures my love of wool and punch needle rug hooking. I created this piece using both 4-cut wool strips with the Oxford fine #10 and 6-cut wool strips with Oxford regular #10. I tried a proddy border to finish it off."

Author's note: There are several good books on the proddy technique, including *Prodded Hooking for a Three-Dimensional Effect* by Gene Shepherd.

Quiet Winter. Advanced Oxford Certified Instructor Kevin LeMoine, Shemogue, New Brunswick, Canada. 13" × 13". [Amy's note: Kevin used 100% polyester polar fleece strips and 100% wool, 2-ply, worsted-weight Briggs & Little Heritage brand yarn. For clarity below, I use "Heritage yarn."] **Tree, *foreground*, and red barn:** Oxford fine #10 and Heritage yarn; **evergreen, second tree, barn, and blue sky:** Oxford fine #13 and Heritage yarn; **barn roof, *foreground*, and white snowbanks:** Oxford fine #10 and 3-cut polar fleece strips; **dark-blue snow:** Oxford fine #14 and 3-cut polar fleece strips; **medium-blue snow:** Oxford fine #13 and 3-cut polar fleece strips; **red barn, mountain, and yellow sky:** Oxford fine #14 and Heritage yarn.

PUNCHING WITH FABRIC STRIPS

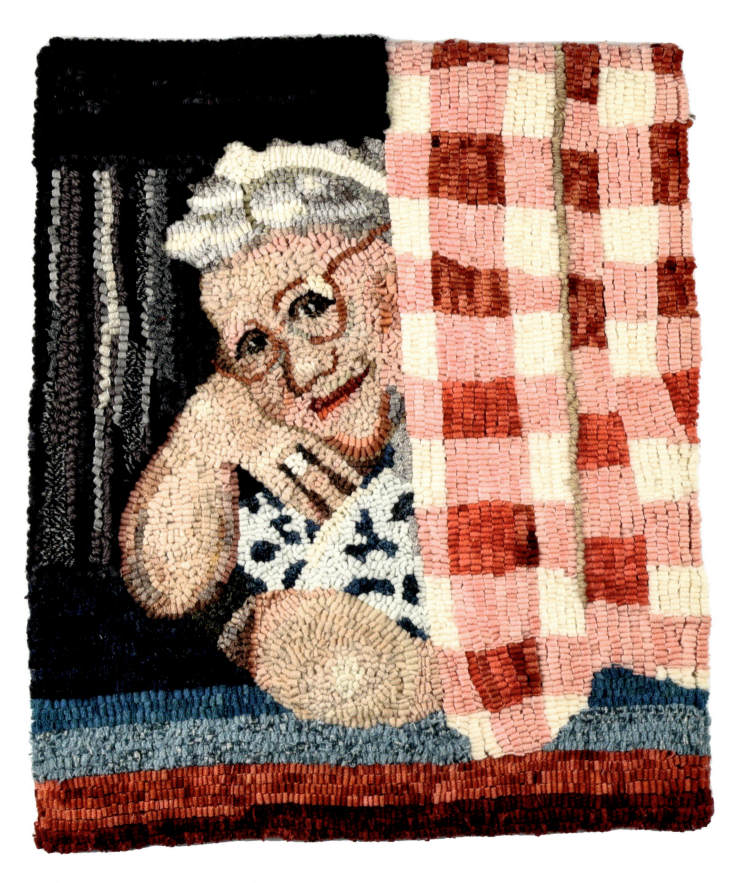

Left: *Mom.* Oxford Certified Instructor Laurel Golden, Sequim, Washington. 15.5" × 18". Hand-dyed wool 6-cut strips and rug-weight yarn with Oxford regular #9. Hand-dyed 4-cut strips with Oxford fine #9 for face and shading.

"I was inspired to do a portrait so chose my mom. My sister had this snapshot on her fridge for ages, so we chose this happy shot (my sister Susan is also making a version). The gingham curtain was not original, but I love the color it gave to the composition."

SOME TIPS ON PUNCHING WITH POLAR FLEECE FROM OXFORD CERTIFIED INSTRUCTOR KEVIN LEMOINE

- My favorite thing about punching with polar fleece is the texture and feel. I prefer regular-weight polar fleece when using 3-cut strips with my fine Oxford Punch Needles and 6-cut strips with my regular Oxford Punch Needles. When I want a coarse look, I use heavyweight polar fleece and 5-cut strips with regular Oxford Punch Needles.

- Be very careful threading your punch needle with 3-cut strips, since there is no grain to polar fleece, and the strips will pull apart. Also, don't pull on your 3-cut strips or they will rip apart; the strength is gained when they are punched into your backing. I test my polar fleece strips in my Oxford Punch Needles for resistance, the same as I do with yarns. It is important to have the right tension to get even loops.

- Polar fleece can dull your cutter head blade, so I suggest using a quilter's mat and rotary cutter. I use my Bolivar Cutter, but caution is required.

- Although I love punching with polar fleece, it is very easy to get discouraged. I recommend starting with a wider cut in a regular Oxford Punch Needle, until you get the feel for it, and then you can move on to a narrower cut in a fine point Oxford Punch Needle.

6
Two-Color Beading Stitch

by Louise Kulp with contributions by Amy Oxford

THE PERFECTLY PAISLEY PROJECT

Perfectly Paisley. 15.75" × 15.75". Oxford regular #10 and 3-ply hand-dyed rug-weight wool yarn. Color plan and execution by Louise Kulp. Designed by Cotey Gallagher.

Perfectly Paisley. 15.75" × 15.75". Oxford fine #14 and worsted-weight yarn to fill in paisleys. Oxford regular #10 and rug-weight yarn for everything else. Color plan and execution by Amy Oxford. Designed by Cotey Gallagher.

Pattern size: 15" × 15"

You will need:

- Monk's cloth size: 24" × 24" or size needed to fit your frame
- 18" × 18" Oxford Gripper Strip Lap Frame
- Oxford Punch Needles #10 regular and #10 fine (optional).

Yarn needed:

- Approximately 20 ounces of rug-weight yarn or a combination of rug-weight and worsted-weight yarn. This is a great project for using leftovers from your stash.

> The pattern is available as a download at www.schiffercraft.com/ intermediate&advancedpunchneedle.

LOUISE'S TWO-COLOR BEADING STITCH

Punch needle rug hooking captured my creative heart nearly two decades ago. I love it for its simplicity, and I love it for its complexity. And even today I am still discovering its nuances and potential for creative expression.

For example, several years ago I was experimenting with new ways to create motion in my work—the sun sparkling on water, wispy clouds drifting across the sky. I also wanted new ways to depict patterns in nature, such as the crackly veins in a fall leaf or the speckled skin of a pear.

I developed what I called my "dotted-line technique" to achieve these special effects and quickly realized it had precedent in fiber arts as beading stitch. Worked in rows with two colors, it gives the appearance of beads or small dots. Rug hooker and dyer Ingrid Hieronimus included beading stitch in her book *Special Effects Using Creative Stitches* (Ragg Tyme Studio, 2014), with diagrams and photographs for working the stitch in traditional rug hooking technique. Crochet and knitting have versions as well—look up "two-color slip stitch" in a knitting-stitch dictionary and you'll see dotted lines all over hats, scarves, and sweaters.

(Knitters also have "bead stitch" and "beaded rib stitch," but those are worked in one color and named for a texture of small raised bumps.)

Beading stitch for punch needle rug hooking can be worked in straight lines and curves. It can be used for outlining or filling in, and to enhance areas of multivalue shading by adding texture and interest. Beading stitch also has tremendous potential for creating eye-catching transitions between the three design elements in rugs: object, background, and border. You can achieve a contemporary graphic look with a row of high-contrast beading, or a subtle, more natural look with colors of similar value.

Legendary knitting author and designer Elizabeth Zimmermann famously used the term "to un-vent" to acknowledge that techniques she discovered likely existed already in the history-of-knitting timeline. I will use it, too, to acknowledge my un-vention of beading stitch for punch needle rug hooking. Surely there are other fiber artists out there achieving the same effect, but my technique—methodical and versatile—meets the needs of my design vision well, and I hope it will meet yours too!

Cotey Gallagher's lively paisley pattern is a veritable playground for beading stitch, and the perfect framework for me to continue my exploration of this special effect in punch needle rug hooking. I used two basic applications of the stitch—outlining objects and making borders with mitered corners—so that readers can focus on learning the technique. You may choose to follow my lead, or you may choose instead to dive right into the deep end and use beading stitch however and wherever you want.

Both of my smaller paisleys are outlined in graceful curves of beading stitch worked in two high-contrast colors: red (or purple) beads and ivory. High-contrast beading results in a sharp "staccato" effect. The outline of my large paisley is softer, since two rows of beading allow for a wider and more subtle transition through similar values of blue, green, and gold, and finally into the neutral background.

The 1" border framing my mat packs six different colors into just three rows of punching. I guess you could say that beading stitch packs a lot of punch! The corners were carefully planned so that all four have the same diagonal miter—an ivory bead in the inside corner, then blue, green, and, last, red in the outside corner. The entire mat is outlined in one solid row of a darker value of Joan Moshimer's Jacobean Bright Red formula at a gauge of six stitches per inch. Practiced punchers know that the two outermost rows of a rug measure six stitches or loops per inch punched in side-by-side rows of monk's cloth. In our mat we accomplish this with one row of beading stitch and one regular solid-color row (look for color C in figure 2).

In a Nutshell

- Bead stitch creates a dotted-line effect that will add interest to your work and make the viewer lean in for a closer look. It can be subtle, with alternating loops of a similar value (a light blue and a light green, for example), or dramatic (alternating loops of black and white).

- Add even more interest by making one bead solid and the other variegated. This will keep one bead color constant while the other changes.

- For that matter, try two variegated yarns together! Multiple rows of bead stitch can be used side by side to create a check pattern (as seen in the border of our Perfectly Paisley Project).

Louise's color palette

Amy's color palette

COLOR PLAN

Louise chose colors from Joan Moshimer's Jacobean Dye Formulas to dye 3-ply wool rug yarn for her mat: #2 Spring Green in six values; #18 Bright Red in six values; #5 Brown Gold, #13 Green Blue, #16 Wild Grape, and #17 Bright Green as solids; and Joan's Background Formula as a spot dye.

Amy chose rug yarns from Violet Jane, Judith Hotchkiss Designs and Dyeworks, and Seal Harbor Rug Company. The Violet Jane Rainbow Trout variegated yarn (*second from top*) creates a dotted line with multicolored dots! Worsted-weight yarns are from Tibet Himalayan Yarn spun from wool and recycled silk (*top*), Violet Jane Barber Pole (*third from top*), and assorted unknown yarns from her stash. The Tibet yarn is the background inside the paisleys. The barber pole is fun because the stripes create a "faux bead stitch." Amy always changes her mind as she goes (it's a given!) and added white and a dull orange rug yarn. She didn't include the little ball of bling (shown on top of corals) because it was too distracting to come to the party.

TECHNIQUE

BEADING STITCH DIAGRAMS

The diagrams below illustrate my way of making two-color beading stitch in punch needle rug hooking. Each square represents an empty hole in the foundation cloth, whether monk's cloth, linen, or rug warp. I punched my Paisley Project by using an Oxford Regular #10 and rug-weight yarn, and Amy punched hers with an Oxford Regular #10 and rug-weight yarn (outside the paisleys) and an Oxford Fine #14 and worsted-weight yarn (inside the paisleys). Figure 1 includes a diagram showing both rug-weight and worsted-weight yarns.

One row of beading stitch takes two steps: a foundation step with color A and a fill-in step with color B. Using rug-weight yarn and a corresponding size of punch needle, a completed row of beading stitch measures six stitches per inch; each color measures three stitches per inch. Lay a foundation row of color A by punching in every fourth hole of monk's cloth. This leaves three empty holes

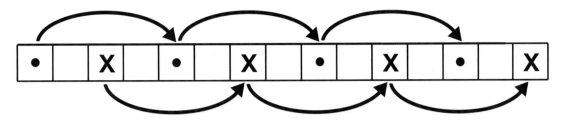

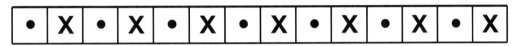

Figure 1. Basic two-color beading stitch for both rug-weight yarn and worsted-weight yarn

between each stitch. Complete the row by punching color B in the middle hole of the three empty holes between every color A stitch. **Make sure you put color B into the *very same row* of monk's cloth as color A.**

For worsted-weight yarn and corresponding finer point punch needle, put color A in every other monk's cloth hole, then fill the empty holes with color B.

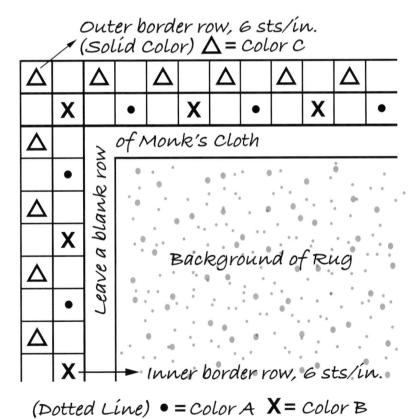

Figure 2. Beaded borders

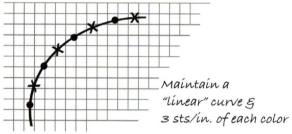

Figure 3. Beading on the curve

Beading-stitch borders have an impressive, complex look that belies their technical simplicity (your friends will ask, "How did you do that?"). Colors can be manipulated to make borders bold or subtle and to make corners that look mitered. Plan ahead to ensure that whatever colors you want to land in the corners do.

Beading stitch is a linear technique, no matter which way your design lines meander. To bead in curved shapes, simply punch each color in turn, following the outline or contour of your shape. Aim for three stitches per inch of each color (six stitches per inch per completed curve), just as you do in straight-line beading.

Steps 1 and 2 with rug yarn (left) and worsted-weight yarn (right) shown from the back

Completed Steps 1 and 2 (front)

170 TWO-COLOR BEADING STITCH

BEAD STITCH BASICS

It's easy when you know how! Just punch two rows of stitches into the same row of monk's cloth holes. **Step 1**: Punch the first color (red). **Step 2**: Punch the second color (green). Use the tip of your finger to gently pull back on your red stitch. Tuck the tip of your punch under the red stitch and then push your punch down all the way.

If you measure (or count) your first row of stitches, you don't have to do so for the second. Just put your punch under the middle of each stitch in the first row.

When using monk's cloth with 12 holes per inch (recommended):

For rug yarn: Use three stitches per inch (punch in every fourth hole).

For worsted-weight yarn: Use six stitches per inch (punch in every other hole).

TWO-COLOR BEADING STITCH

ADDITIONAL TIPS

If you want your row of beads to look truly "dotted," poke the colors into alignment (A, B, A, B, etc.) before you surround them with more loops.

Turn your work over and check the front side regularly. Poke as you go or it will be a huge job at the end!

Because a row of beading stitch is slightly thicker than a normal, one-color row—essentially, you're putting one yarn on top of another—you may wish to leave a little extra space than usual between beading-stitch rows and adjacent areas.

Color B loops tend to stand a bit taller than their fellow color A loops. If you want colors of equal prominence, insert the tips of *closed* embroidery scissors and pull up slightly on color A loops after the row is complete.

Speed up your work by keeping two punch needles threaded, one for each color.

Try using a variegated yarn for one of your two colors. It will make it look like you've worked much harder than you really have!

Many punchers don't count holes as they punch, but we do suggest counting for the border.

An electric sweater depiller works beautifully to clean up your work and make your colors sharper and more defined.

In addition to the applications shown here, I have used beading stitch in my punch needle rug hooking designs to make a wicker basket, the center of a daisy, the contour of an apple, and the trails left by a shooting star in the night sky. I also have used it to add texture to areas of eight-value shading and to miter the corners of a faux wooden frame. The more I use this very special effect, the more I appreciate its versatility and creative potential. I see possibilities *everywhere*. Dive right in and give beading stitch a try!

Louise made this sampler to illustrate ways to use the bead stitch. Note how the trail behind the shooting star is made by using bead stitch loops.

BEAD STITCH ENVY

by Amy Oxford

The first time I saw the bead stitch, I didn't know what it was called, but I knew I wanted to try it! I saw a gorgeous traditionally hooked rug in an exhibit that included one single crisp row of black-and-white loops that looked like a dotted line. How on earth did they do it? I asked a traditional rug-hooking friend, and they told me the rug hooker held two strips of wool fabric under the rug and alternated pulling up loops with their rug hook, first a black one, then a white one, etc. My hopes were dashed because this method wouldn't work with the punch needle. I could thread a black and a white strand of yarn together in my punch, but every loop I punched would be a mix of black and white. I love to punch with strips, but two strips of 6-cut or 8-cut strips would be too thick to thread through the punch at once.

I've been scratching my head for over ten years and have asked many punchers if they could figure it out, to no avail. And then Eureka! My ingenious friend Louise Kulp solved the mystery! I asked Louise if she'd like to write this article with me, and she was as excited as I was. She agreed to write the directions, and we decided to both punch the same piece. Louise's directions wound up being all that was needed for the entire article, and all I've added are some additional tips at the end. The credit is all hers.

With Louise's directions as my guide, I couldn't wait to start. Ten years of pent-up bead stitch envy came flooding out of my punch! Inspired by her description of Cotey Gallagher's Paisley pattern as a "veritable playground for beading stitch" and her encouragement to dive right in, I was off. This was a super-fun project and I hope you'll dive right in as well!

. A Note from Amy .

WHAT I LEARNED FROM LOUISE AND FROM MAKING THE PERFECTLY PAISLEY PROJECT

- I learned how to make the bead stitch both with rug-weight and worsted-weight yarns and discovered that it was even more fun and had more possible applications than I could have imagined! Now I want to add a little bead stitch to everything, even if it's just using two similar colors to add a bit of dappling here and there.

EXAMPLES OF MULTIPLE TECHNIQUES

Tarot Rug. Oxford Certified Instructor Christie Beniston, Solana Beach, California. 36" × 36". Punched with rug-weight wool yarn. **Background:** Oxford regular #10. **Earth elements:** Oxford regular #9. **Lettering:** To make the quote more readable, Christie first punched the letters using an Oxford regular #10, then took it all out and re-punched with an Oxford regular #9 to make the letters show up more clearly. (This is called using a "space keeper.")

"I collaborated with my daughter Isa on the design for this rug, which was inspired by the tarot. All four earth elements are represented along with a quotation from F. D. Graves's description of the World card in *Windows of Tarot*: 'Seek not the world, for at this moment it is spinning just beneath you.' The quote brought perspective to an uncertain time and is a reminder to live in and practice gratitude for the present moment."

The Fan Interpretation of Artist Modigliani. Oxford Certified Instructor Carol Gaylor, Lindsay, Ontario, Canada. 20" × 25".

"The simple lines of the painting by Italian artist Amedeo Modigliani inspired me to use different mediums and take on a piece of recycled wool. I overdyed it several times to create the background." Oxford regular #9 with cut strips of wool, sari silk ribbon, and wool rug-weight yarn.

Welcome to the Vortex. Advanced Oxford Certified Instructor Cotey Gallagher, Salisbury, Vermont. 40" × 20". Oxford regular #9 with wool rug yarn. Grid lines punched with stem stitch and "legal jumping" (see page 29 in *Punch Needle Rug Hooking* by Amy Oxford). Gradation of values in the center of the "hole" uses mock shading in alternating rows of gray.

"This rug is my take on the common optical illusion of the sinkhole. I made this rug for my front entryway as a joke because I have a friend that says when they visit our home, it's like they got sucked into a vortex (of comfort and laziness)."

Mandala Chair Pads Set. Advanced Oxford Certified Instructor Cotey Gallagher, Salisbury, Vermont. 15" × 15". Oxford regular #8 with wool rug yarn. Stem stitch used on all single lines. Braid ties were whip stitched onto the corners to secure chair pad to chair. Blunt yarn/tapestry needle used for whip stitch.

"This will be a set of six chair pads when complete. All the same colors are used in each of the chair pads but are placed in different elements of the design in each piece. This was an exercise to show the importance of color placement and how it affects the overall look of the entire piece."

EXAMPLES OF MULTIPLE TECHNIQUES 179

7

Shading with Yarn: A Painter's Approach

FEATURING COLLEEN SOLOMOS FAULKNER

by Amy Oxford | Photos by Jim Faulkner

When Oxford Certified Instructor Colleen Solomos Faulkner and I met, there was a lot of laughter and oohing and aahing on my part as Colleen showed me her basement studio, yarns, rugs, and dye kitchen. Her backdrop was a wall of cubbies brimming with sumptuous yarns, and it appeared that no two skeins were alike. I wasn't sure what I was seeing when she brought out armloads of white cardboard cards, each one covered with single strands of yarn. She has made one of these sample cards for every rug she's ever made. Each card is neatly labeled with the rug name and includes notes about the project. Here's where the awe-inspiring part comes in . . . Colleen has made over 200 rugs and has kept a yarn samples, notes, and a photo of every single one!

For me, as the person responsible for making thousands of Oxford Punch Needles, the thing that made me wildly happy? Colleen has used only ONE Oxford Punch Needle to create all 200-plus rugs! The punch is a #14 fine Mini, and you can tell it has a lot of miles on it by the worn patina. "Every rug I've ever made has been with this 14; she's my old friend! It's not going to stop! It's probably a 14½ now!" Colleen swears that her needle has gotten better with age, saying, "It goes through the monk's cloth like butter." She's very protective of her punch! "I've had people try to walk off with it. So I can't lay it down—it goes in my pocket all the time."

There are three things about Colleen Faulkner's punching that surprised me. The first is that she almost never pulls out her work and redoes it. The second? She doesn't color-plan ahead of time. And the third? She punches the background first. When I learned these things and more during our interview, it was clear to me that she was coming at this from a different angle than I had ever seen before.

At the beginning of each Oxford Punch Needle Teacher Certification Workshop, I ask my students to write down their goals for the future. In Colleen's class in June 2014, Colleen wrote, "I would like to teach, learn, and grow a business into something that's profitable, something that is searched out because of a great product and network of great people that love rugs and yarns. Also to have a line of wool, long term."

Colleen didn't waste any time! A month after becoming certified, she asked her classmate, Patricia (Pat) Merritt, from Green Valley, Arizona, to teach her to dye yarn. Colleen also began teaching punch needle rug hooking right away and made special commissions (including a rug for the governor of Missouri, a portrait of the governor's dog that hung proudly in the portrait room of the Missouri statehouse). Colleen honed her dyeing skills, and her students bought her yarn as fast as she could dye it. Bolstered by her success and sticking to her long-term goals, Colleen officially started her own yarn company in 2018. Pat's nickname for Colleen in their dyeing sessions was "Whackadoo," so when Colleen needed a business name, "Whackadoo Yarns" came to mind.

Poppies. Front. Oxford Certified Instructor Colleen Faulkner, Jefferson City, Missouri. 24" × 36". Oxford fine #10 and 14. Hand-dyed Whackadoo worsted-weight rug yarn.

"This was my Oxford Certified Instructor certification rug. The background used the Oxford fine #14 and the poppies were punched with an Oxford fine #10, using many shades of reds to make the poppy appear to set up off the background. On the edges, I used silk strings in different colors to add a bit of surprise to the eyes."

Cocktails Anyone? (front). Oxford Certified Instructor Colleen Faulkner, Jefferson City, Missouri. 21" × 36". Oxford fine #14 and hand-dyed Whackadoo worsted-weight rug yarn.

"I came up with the idea that I would like a simple kitchen rug that used citrus fruits. I used different cuts of fruit, whether whole or sliced, so that the coloring could be beautiful! Shading is huge for me; I love to show that if you break down any item into sections and focus only on color selection piece by piece, it makes making beautiful pieces easy."

Colleen Faulkner's rugs have a distinct look, a style all their own. Here's how she does it: (1) She has her own artistic style and design sensibility. (2) She uses only her Whackadoo 3-ply worsted-weight yarn. (3) She always works with an Oxford fine #14, with occasional accents and details using an Oxford fine #10 and #13. (4) She doesn't use the conventional stitch size and row spacing recommended in the directions that come with the Oxford Punch Needle (punching in every hole, skipping a row of empty holes). Instead, Colleen punches in every *other* hole—and does *not* leave a row of empty holes. Both methods produce the same number of loops per square inch (approximately 70–80), but her spacing produces a unique look on the front and back. Colleen is the first to admit that her stitch sizes are not always the same, "because you have to stagger them sometimes, like laying bricks." (5) Because Colleen doesn't leave a row of empty holes, and she whips all her rugs instead of having a white monk's cloth hem showing, her rugs are reversible. (6) She uses fingering shading almost everywhere. (7) She uses a LOT of colors in each object. For example, a rooster might have 45 different colors! (8) And here's the key difference: she dyes and prepares her yarn specifically for shading.

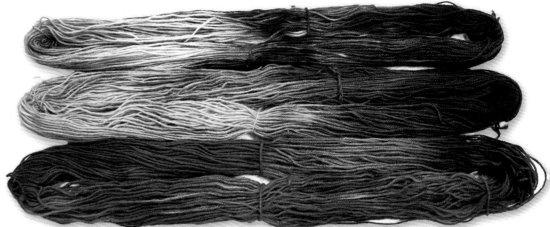

Colleen pours dye on each end of the skein so the ends are the darkest. The two colors meet in the middle to create a third color.

DYEING

Colleen now offers a staggering 860 yarn colors that she hand-dyes herself. Her base yarn is 3-ply worsted-weight 100% New Zealand wool and is a creamy-white natural color. She uses PRO Chemical dyes, and, believe it or not, she uses only twelve PRO Chem colors to create all of her formulas. (For curious dyers, those colors are Black, Turquoise, Forest Green, Sun Yellow, Golden Yellow, Magenta, Bright Red, Jolly Red, Bright Orange, Navy, Brilliant Blue, and National Blue.) Colleen relies on the three primary colors, black, and a few supporting colors to create her entire palette. She thinks that all her yarns work harmoniously together because they spring from the same base colors. When you look at her rugs, I think you'll agree that not only do they work together, but they play together!

Her brilliance is in the *way* she uses them. "Before any of this," she explains, "I painted with watercolor." When she started making punched rugs, she wondered, "How do you make the fiber coloring behave like watercolor? There's got to be a way!" She explained that, as a watercolor artist, she learned how the paint traveled and was affected by the movement of the water. Colleen experimented with dyeing her yarn and found that the only way she could get the effect she wanted was to convert her powder dyes into liquid form. Colleen "dip-dyes" her yarn in stainless-steel lasagna pans on a gas cooktop. This involves putting a skein of yarn in the pan and pouring a solution of dye on each end. She often uses a different color on each end as well. The liquid dye flows through the yarn, spreading the dyes in a similar way that water spreads and dilutes paint. Because she pours the dye on the ends, they are the darkest, while the colors get lighter as they spread to the middle. The real fun happens when the two colors meet and form a third color. Colleen grins and says, "That's where the beauty of that magic comes in." Like an alchemist, Colleen has successfully turned fiber into a watercolor palette. When she wants a more solid look, she also dyes yarn in a dye pot on the stovetop.

SHADING

With pot dyeing, you dye multiple skeins, each one a different shade from light to dark. Colleen says, "I can have 7–12 shades in the same exact color on one skein. So the shading is automatic. One shade feeds into another, feeds into another, feeds into . . . well, you know what I mean! Then you can fussy-cut them." I asked what she meant by "fussy cutting," and she explained that she often cuts strands from sections of the skein to get the specific colors and shades she needs.

When working with her "watercolor skeins," Colleen explains her process: "I don't control it. I just let the yarn do what it does. It speaks for

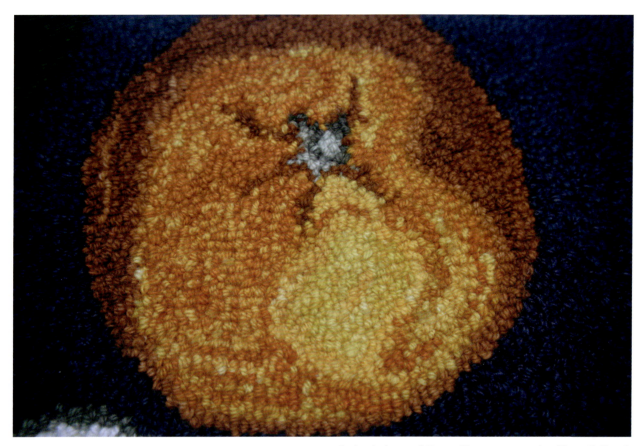

Cocktails Anyone? Front. Close-up example of how Colleen's Whackadoo yarns "do all the work." She drew a diagram for herself to show where she wanted to put her lights and darks and took it from there. The whole orange is punched using one skein of her "watercolor yarn."

itself. The yarn does all the work." Colleen has leftover-yarn "grab bags" that are her go-to source for additional colors. "I grab whatever I grab; it goes wherever it goes." Remember, she can't go wrong because all of her colors work together.

COLLEEN AT THE RUG FRAME

When Colleen starts a new rug, she dives right in. "I don't spend all this time gathering and putting all the stuff together," she says. She starts by punching the background (a method she uses in painting). Though Colleen has the big picture in mind as she punches, she focuses on one small area at a time. "I'm just looking at a 1-inch square. I work inch by inch, like a puzzle. It's just a little space that I work on. That's all I see, so I fill in one little space, then another little space, then another. I pick a color, fill it in, move on, pick a color, and put it in there." "Nothing is ever

> *"I don't control it. I just let the yarn do what it does. It speaks for itself. The yarn does all the work."*

186 SHADING WITH YARN: A PAINTER'S APPROACH

stressful," she explains. "It's wool. You know what I mean? It's yarn. Just pick something. There are 50,000 million shades of green, and you're focusing on the fact that you want an olive green?" Perhaps this is a Missouri saying, but I loved it when Colleen said, "Oh gosh, it would be a bad world of hurt if I had to just find one!" Colleen laughs and says, "Now you are into the head of Colleen Faulkner. And it's scary, is it not?"

Colleen often punches in front of TV and tells me she's easily distracted, especially when it comes to sports. She describes the scenario that many TV-watching punchers know well: "When you're watching a Cubs game and they do something stupid and you veer off the path! Or a movie, and you don't pay attention? You're just punching and you look down and you realize you just left a big hole, a big empty space."

"I use that as a moment to pick something else, to pick anything; it doesn't matter. These are shading moments. A moment to be brilliant! I pick a different color and put it in those spaces. I fill it in with something else, another color. It doesn't even mean a value. Let's say you're doing a green and you left that hole . . . put yellow in there, brown in there, orange in there, tan in there, anything! I pick a lighter color, a darker color, a completely off-the-grid different color." As a teacher she laments, "It scares people to do that!"

Colleen's Pro Tip #1: Multistranding. With this technique you start by separating your yarn. For example, if you have a 3-ply yarn, separate it into three individual strands. You can then switch out one or two of the strands and replace them with different colors. (You can see this in the birch trees in the close-up of her rug *Great Grandma Helga*.)

Great Grandma Helga (back). Oxford Certified Instructor Colleen Faulkner, Jefferson City, Missouri. 60" × 48". Oxford fine #10, 13, and 14 and hand-dyed Whackadoo worsted-weight rug yarn.

"This is a rug that has many things going on. It was adapted from a Russian lacquer box. I changed many items from being scary to what I liked. For example, I turned spiderwebs into a basket of yarn. The thatched roof, horse's mane, and braids on the woman are all done with a longer loop. The trees in the background were punched with two strands: one strand of black and one strand of gray, to make them look like birch. I tried to blend many plain yarns into three strands of different colors. This made the mushrooms and plants come alive."

Great Grandma Helga (back). Close-up of birch tree branches to show her multistranding technique (see the pro tip).

Colleen's Pro Tip #2: Punching in layers. Colleen always punches with the Oxford fine #14 Mini. If she wants to add extra dimension, she "layers" her work by punching on top of these short loops with the taller loops made with an Oxford fine #10. She uses a thin piece of yarn for this extra layer. (You can see this in the thistle over the rabbits in her rug *The Guardian*.)

The Guardian (back). Oxford Certified Instructor Colleen Faulkner, Jefferson City, Missouri. 54" × 40". Oxford fine #10 and 14. Hand-dyed Whackadoo worsted-weight rug yarn. Design adapted with permission from watercolorist, artist, and illustrator Jackie Morris.

"Each year, I try to push myself to be better as an artist and dyer. This rug changed everything. To flow like watercolors, the background of white fading into the color of the outline of the polar bear had to be created in the dye process. This rug is punched with the Oxford fine #10 and #14 because I punched it into layers to look like an embroidered rug. The thistle over the rabbits is made with a fine piece of yarn punched over the top of the rabbits, as is the stitching on her dress. It all had to be built up in layers."

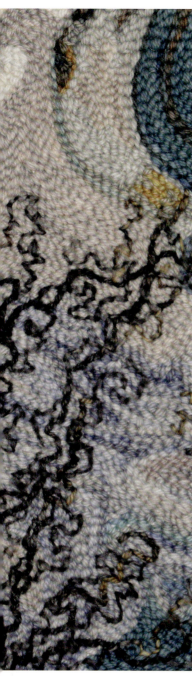

The Guardian (back). Close-up to show Colleen's "punching layers" technique (see the pro tip).

Midnight Delivery (back). Oxford Certified Instructor Colleen Faulkner, Jefferson City, Missouri. 35" × 22". Oxford fine #14 and hand-dyed Whackadoo worsted-weight rug yarn. Design adapted from a 1930s vintage postcard.

"Santa's green coat that flowed in the breeze was made by using three different colors of green to show folds in the fabric. The snow shadows were made using blues with walnut hues, giving it an aged look."

SHADING WITH YARN: A PAINTER'S APPROACH   191

VINTAGE POSTCARD SERIES

Colleen collects vintage postcards that were printed between 1910 and 1920. Her series is an homage to the artists, most of whom were not given credit. She buys the postcards online from antique collectors and on eBay. Some of the postcards are worth thousands of dollars. Colleen is fascinated by the fact that so many have survived, and laughed when she told me, "Most of the cards I've collected are addressed to 'Mabel.' I don't know why; I guess it was a popular name at that time!"

Decorating Christmas (front). Oxford Certified Instructor Colleen Faulkner, Jefferson City, Missouri. 43" × 31". Oxford fine #14 and hand-dyed Whackadoo worsted-weight rug yarn. Design adapted from a 1930s vintage postcard.

"I am a lover of the Christmas season. My vintage postcard series pays tribute to the artists that designed them and the talent they had. The rug was punched using subtle shades of the same color in the background, while using bright and vibrant colors for the children in the front to make the design look three-dimensional."

Chicks and Lilies (front). *Oxford Certified Instructor* Colleen Faulkner, Jefferson City, Missouri. 29" × 36". Oxford fine #14 and hand-dyed Whackadoo worsted-weight rug yarn. Design adapted from a 1930s vintage postcard. Collection of Amy Oxford.

This rug is a great example of Colleen's "inch by inch" punching approach. You can really see the detail she puts into every inch. Colleen generously gifted me this rug to thank me for being her teacher. It's both humbling and wonderful when a student's talent takes off in a new way, in a creative and different direction with skills you never could have imagined!

SHADING WITH YARN: A PAINTER'S APPROACH

Hippity Hop (back). Oxford Certified Instructor Colleen Faulkner, Jefferson City, Missouri. 27" × 24". Oxford fine #14 and hand-dyed Whackadoo worsted-weight rug yarn. Design adapted from a 1930s vintage postcard.

"Another vintage postcard for the Easter season, 31 different colors used to give lots of shading details. Shading for this rug was about the yarn. It was dyed then overdyed with walnut to give the yarn an aged look. I love the old feeling it has."

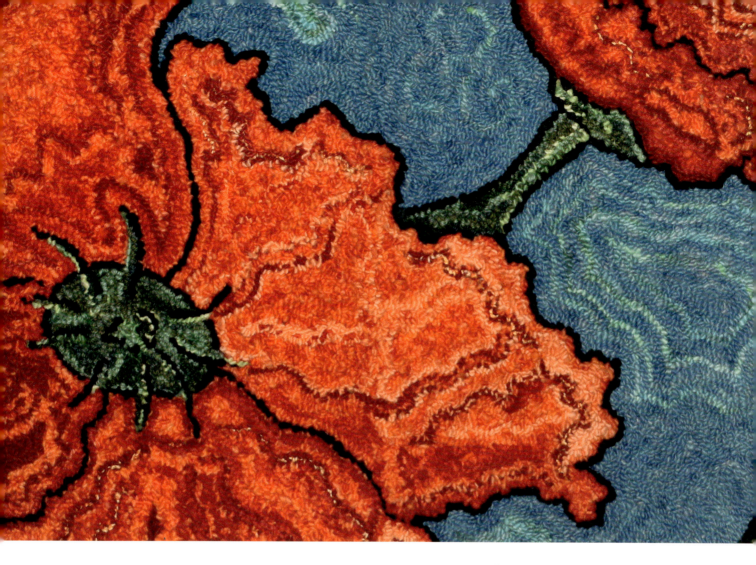

I asked Colleen if she had any advice for our readers. It occurred to me after the fact that her approach was a union of watercolor and the pointillism of Georges Seurat. To get us all to lighten up, she laughed and gently scolded: "They're dots! When you punch, you're only making a dot! Just get in there and punch it. Put this here, put that there, you know? It's not difficult. The punch has to go in and out, in and out. That's what you need to focus on. People try so hard to be perfect. They should just enjoy what they're doing; that's when the magic happens."

Colleen Faulkner

— 8 —
Telling Stories with Your Punch Needle

by Margaret Mitchell

You may like the idea of designing a rug that captures a special event, or a family activity you want to remember—but, like me, you don't feel you have the artistic talent or computer skills to create such a rug. This section is for you!

In the following pages, you will learn all the tricks you need to succeed in designing a rug that conveys a people-focused story. (If you are good at sophisticated computer graphics programs, of if you know someone who is, then you will see that you can do most of what is described here on the computer easily and quickly—no need for photocopies.)

I particularly enjoy designing rugs that capture our experiences in my part of the world, such as the ones about making maple syrup and cutting ice that you see here. I am an Oxford Certified Instructor, and a member of The Oxford Punch Needle Instructors Guild (OPNIG), The International Guild of Handhooking Rugmakers (TIGHR), the Ontario Hooking Craft Guild (OHCG), and the Olde Forge and Glebe rug hooking groups in Ottawa.

I really wanted to make a series of rugs that told the story of traditions at our 31-Mile Lake in the Upper Gatineau area of Quebec (Canada) as a way to preserve this history for coming generations. I was inspired in this idea by the work of a Canadian artist, Nokomis. In her paintings she vividly tells us stories of growing up in rural northern Canada.

Once I was thinking along these lines, it occurred to me that I could also adopt, in modified form, something of the style of another Canadian artist whose work I particularly like, Ted Harrison.

Both Nokomis and Ted Harrison paint fairly simply drawn people (outlined in black) and fairly simple landscapes, telling a story with just enough detail to bring the scene alive. This is just what is needed in a rug: enough detail to convey the activity, but not more than you can fit into your rug design.

You might be interested in having a look at their work—it could inspire you in the same way it did me. You can find more about Nokomis at https://www.native-art-in-canada.com/nokomis.html, and Ted Harrison at https://tedharrison.ca/.

To illustrate the process of designing a rug in this way, I will use the *Cutting Ice: 31-Mile Lake* rug as an example.

Cutting Ice. Oxford Certified Instructor Margaret Mitchell, Ottawa, Ontario, Canada. 37" × 25". Oxford regular #10, wool rug yarn. *Photo credit: Anne-Marie Littenberg*

Cutting large blocks of ice out of the lake and saving them for summer refrigeration was once a necessity and is now a unique treat. They were originally cut by handsaw, but a long-bladed chainsaw now makes the job easier. The block is floated to the edge of the lake and pulled out with large tongs. A rope runs from the truck, up over a pulley at the top of the chute, and back down the hill to the lake. This rope is wrapped around the block and the truck backs up on the frozen lake, pulling the ice up the chute. The ice is stacked in the icehouse belowground, packed in sawdust, ready to be used come summer.

You will need:

- As many photographs as possible that show the setting and, most importantly, people in active positions engaged in the activity. This will give you a way of showing people in motion in your rug design.
- Access to a photocopier and ideally a computer
- Fine (*not* extra-fine) black permanent markers (e.g., Sharpies)
- Soft pencil and high quality eraser
- One or two sheets of erasable, opaque graph paper with nonreproducible grid that is large enough to draw your half-scale image. You may need to tape together more than one sheet to make this size. The number of squares per inch is not important (graph paper makes it significantly easier to measure and draw on the square). I use Canson's Graph and Layout Paper with nonreproducible blue grid.
- Transfer medium, such as "red dot" (to copy your design onto the backing you will use)

STEP 1: SELECT THE PHOTOGRAPHS

The first step is to think about the event or activity you want to portray. Think about what people are doing and the setting in which the action is taking place. The more photographs you have of people engaged in the event, the better, whether they are actively doing something or standing by watching. You will want to take (or find in your archive) as many action shots as possible so that you have a wide range of poses to choose from for your characters.

Figure 1

Figure 2

Figure 3

Figure 4

Figure 5

Figure 6

STEP 2: ROUGH COMPOSITION

Once you have assembled the photographs you want to use, pick out the ones that best capture the setting and the activity. I chose a photo of the hillside with trees (figure 1), the chute up the hill to the icehouse (figure 2), cutting the ice with the chainsaw (figure 3), pulling a block of ice out of the water, ready to be pulled up the chute (figure 4), and one of the people watching the activities (figure 5) and the truck that pulls the ice up the chute to the icehouse (figure 6). You can also "borrow" images from another time or event that fit your design, as I did with the dogs here.

TELLING STORIES WITH YOUR PUNCH NEEDLE

Pick the photograph(s) that best convey the overall setting. Don't worry about the details—your focus here is on the general scene. These one or two photographs will start you thinking about how you want to place the people in the landscape. In this example, I started with figures 1 and 2, which give some detail of the trees on the hill and of the overall setting.

Next, look for people in interesting poses; can you imagine them in the scene you are creating in the landscape you have chosen? Don't worry about whether they are in proportion to the landscape or in the right place—you can fix that later. In this example, I chose figures 3, 4, and 5. Are there any other features of the activity that need to be in your rug? In this case, the truck has an important role to play, so I chose figure 6.

Now it is time to bring out graph paper, pencil, and ruler. If you are not able to find opaque graph and layout paper, use paper that you can see through that can also withstand a fair amount of erasing! It will make the final step much easier if you use paper with nonreproducible grid lines. Using a ruler and following the grid lines, draw a rectangle that is *exactly half* the size you want your finished rug to be.

Then *very* roughly (using squares or oblongs to stand in for the actual image) sketch in the position and size of the elements you plan to take from the photographs you have chosen to use. You are not aiming for a finished drawing, just the general placement and size of the various features. Keep in mind that you are not necessarily looking to re-create the exact scene—feel free to move people and objects around to get a pleasing balance of elements and to simplify your design so that it can be punched. For example, each element needs to be large enough to include the detail needed to tell the story, but not more. You will thank yourself for this simplicity once you begin punching!

Your sketch will give you the relative size of each element of the design. Remember that your sketch is *half* the size of your finished rug. Measure and record the size of each image, top to bottom.

STEP 3: PREPARE THE SELECTED PHOTOGRAPHS

Once you have decided on the images to use, get the photographs ready:

Resize the part of each photograph you want to use, increasing it or decreasing it according to the sketch you made. In the case of the background, adjust only the key elements; you can draw a simple version of the rest of the scene around them. You can determine the percentage to increase or decrease each image on the photocopier, using the following method, or simply use a proportion calculator app on your computer or smartphone.

Figure 7

TO CALCULATE INCREASE (ENLARGEMENT):

New image size divided by old image size times 100.

For example, if your image is 3" high and you would like it to be 5", then your calculation would be $(5 \div 3) \times 100 = 166$. This is the % enlargement you would enter into the photocopier.

TO CALCULATE DECREASE (REDUCTION):

Old image size divided by new image size times 100.

For example, if your image is 5" high and you would like it to be 3", then your calculation would be $(3 \div 5) \times 100 = 60$. This is the % reduction you would enter into the photocopier.

Once you have the size you want, it will be much easier in the next steps if you first edit them to black and white, with the highest possible contrast.

With a fine-tip black marker, outline key elements of the person or the object you want to include in your design, both the outer lines and any other details needed to define the subject (figure 7). The darker the line relative to the rest of the image, the easier the next step will be.

Roughly cut off any excess paper around the image you are using. Don't cut exactly, because you will need some space on the outside of the black outline.

STEP 4: TRANSFER THE PREPARED IMAGES TO THE HALF-SCALE DRAWING

This is when it is handy to have a good-quality eraser!

Arrange the images you have prepared *under* the opaque graph paper. Move the pieces around until you have a pleasing balance and have created a scene that looks and feels "right." During this process you may realize that you would like something to be smaller or larger than you originally thought—just repeat the process in step 3 (above). Using the "almost-right-sized" version as your starting point will make this much easier.

Once you have the design set, simply trace the images through onto the opaque graph paper, using a soft pencil. Take care to keep the images in position as you work.

STEP 5: COMPLETE THE HALF-SCALE DRAWING

With all the key features of your design in place, now draw in the background spaces, using the original photograph of the scene as a guide, but simplifying it as much as possible.

Once you are satisfied with your drawing, finish by tracing all of your pencil lines with a fine-tip black marker. This will give the best result for the final step (a full-sized photocopy).

STEP 6: FINALIZE THE DESIGN PATTERN

Enlarge the half-scale drawing to full size. By far the easiest and best way to do this is to find a photocopy business near you that can produce large images. However, you can also do the enlargement on a regular photocopier by folding your design into sections, copying each folded panel at 200%, and then taping the pieces together. If you do this, it is critical that you *pay careful attention* to placing each folded piece on the photocopier in *exactly* the same position (Can you guess this is the voice of experience?).

And at last, you are now ready to transfer your pattern onto the backing of your choice (preferably monk's cloth), using whichever method works well for you. I trace the design onto "red dot" transfer medium and then onto monk's cloth. Remember, when working with the original Oxford Punch Needle, you will be transferring the pattern backward.

A reminder: The colors in your original photographs can be a useful guide, but don't feel you have to follow them exactly—you may feel adventuresome and want to use colors the way Ted Harrison does, or be like Nokomis and have a slightly less stylized landscape but still keep it simple. Or, you may want to change the colors of the clothes people are wearing to achieve better balance in your final rug. I follow Amy's rule of thumb on color planning: think about how you will include light, bright, dark, and dull.

I hope you enjoy designing rugs that tell a story. I know you, and your rug's viewers, will appreciate the memories your rug preserves for the future.

Left: *Making Maple Syrup.* Oxford Certified Instructor Margaret Mitchell, Ottawa, Ontario, Canada. 37" × 25". **Snow:** Oxford regular #10, three strands in one needle with wool worsted-weight yarn; **outline of landscapes:** Oxford regular #10, 6-cut wool fabric strips; **fire and dogs:** Oxford fine #13 and #14, sculpting with worsted-weight yarn; **remaining sections:** Oxford regular #10, wool rug yarn.

In spring, when daytime temperatures are above freezing and nighttime ones below, the sap begins to run and it's time to tap the maple trees. We hang the buckets (some with blue lids) and then collect the sap (the person with the container on a sled), and the boiling begins. It takes 40 quarts of sap to make 1 quart of syrup, so there is lots of time to stand around tending the fire. The lake is still frozen, but the snow has begun melting, exposing autumn's fallen leaves. The dogs, Miro and Dasha, are having great fun. This is the first rug I designed myself! It is my "certification rug," the final requirement for becoming an Oxford Certified Instructor.

Shore Lunch. Oxford Certified Instructor Margaret Mitchell, Ottawa, Ontario, Canada. 37" × 25". Oxford regular #10, wool rug yarn. *Photo credit: Jim Mitchell*

A tradition at 31-Mile Lake is fishing with a guide who both knows where the fish are biting, and prepares "shore lunch." The ritual for shore lunch is unchanging: start a fire in the cement fire pit, clean and fillet the fish (feeding the entrails to the resident old snapping turtle), cut potato sticks and onion rings, and melt a pound of lard in an enormous frying pan on the fire and cook the meal in it, starting with a pound of bacon, then french fries and onion rings, and finally the fish. Serve with ketchup and baked beans, rounded off with maple sugar tarts and boiled coffee. Delicious!

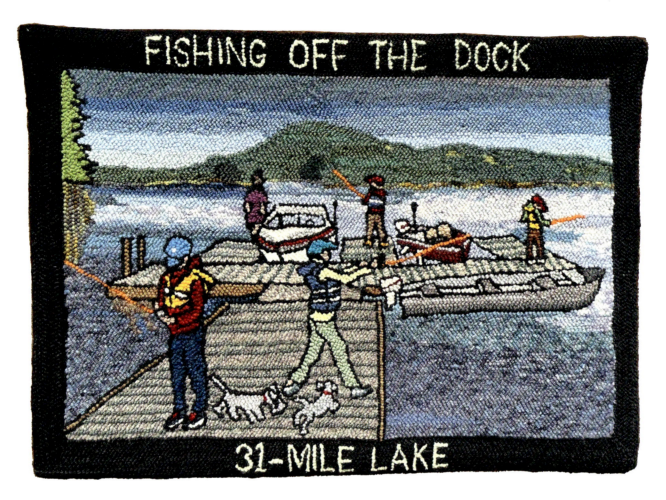

Fishing off the Dock. Oxford Certified Instructor Margaret Mitchell, Ottawa, Ontario, Canada. 37" × 25". Oxford regular #10, wool rug yarn. *Photo credit: Jim Mitchell*

Our grandsons love fishing off the dock, and they are often rewarded by catching a large bass that has been lingering in the shade of the boats or the dock. This rug marks a shift toward a less stylized background, moving away somewhat from the Ted Harrison sweeping contours to a more detailed depiction of the scene.

Picking Chanterelles. Oxford Certified Instructor Margaret Mitchell, Ottawa, Ontario, Canada. 37" × 25". Oxford regular #10, wool rug yarn. *Photo credit: Jim Mitchell*

What joy it is to venture into the forest and be rewarded by the sight of a new patch of chanterelle mushrooms, their golden heads peeping out from the dull forest floor. The locations of chanterelle patches are well-guarded family secrets! The collecting basket has two sides, one for mushrooms we know are safe, and the other for ones to be checked more carefully once home. Everyone helps pick and enjoys the resulting feast.

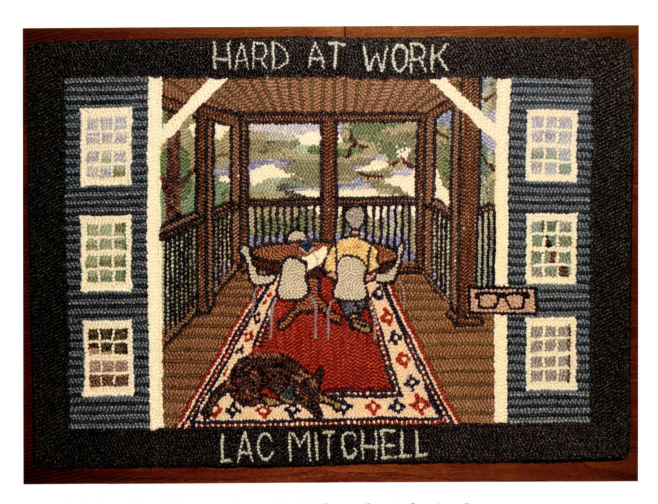

Hard at Work. Oxford Certified Instructor Margaret Mitchell, Ottawa, Ontario, Canada. 37" × 25". Oxford regular #10, wool rug yarn. *In the collection of Richard Stursberg; photo credit: Jim Mitchell*

This rug was commissioned by a friend who spent one summer at his cottage writing at a table on his screen porch. Ideally, he wanted to have both the exterior and interior of his cottage included. This created a design challenge, as did the oriental rug! I was happy to be able to include his dog, Gracie. Are you wondering about the mysterious sign with the eyeglass frames? It was the final sign in a series directing arriving visitors where to turn; the rest of the signposts have disappeared, but the one by the cottage remains.

Sharing Good Times. Oxford Certified Instructor Margaret Mitchell, Ottawa, Ontario, Canada. 37" × 25". Oxford regular #10, wool rug yarn. *In the collection of Morin/Temnikov; photo credit: Jim Mitchell*

When this rug was commissioned, the only instruction was to indicate exactly where the finished rug would hang. I wanted to design a rug that would belong on that dining-room wall and be a happy reminder of the enjoyable evenings spent around that table together, should our friends ever move house. This rug is hanging on the designated wall, and then one more time in the rug itself—a rug in a rug in a rug. It was fun to do, although a challenge to dye the wool to come close to the actual wall color, since too great a difference would be uncomfortably obvious. I now have many different blue greens to use in future rugs!

Margaret Mitchell

TELLING STORIES WITH YOUR PUNCH NEEDLE

3D APPROACHES

Featuring Judith Hotchkiss

Advanced Oxford Certified Instructor Judith Hotchkiss from Deer Isle, Maine, punched these waterbirds by using an Oxford regular #10 and 3-ply wool rug-weight yarn. She made her *Great Blue Heron* into a dummy board. Dummy boards originated in the early 17th century and are traditionally flat figures that have been oil-painted in the trompe l'oeil style to make them look realistic. They are life sized or smaller and placed around the home, often in front of fireplaces or in hallways.

Judith also punched a loon, wood duck, swan, and Canada goose to create stuffed three-dimensional decoys. She punched the front side of her birds, used wool fabric for the back, and placed a flat gusset on the bottom so they would stand up properly.

Great Blue Heron. Judith Hotchkiss, Deer Isle, Maine. 20" × 44". Oxford regular #10, 3-ply wool rug yarn.

"This heron practically punched itself. Once I started I could not stop, and it was great fun using multiple values of the rug yarn to create feathers and wings. The challenge was in the finishing. Originally planned as a freestanding stuffed bird, it evolved into a dummy board as a solution to its fine legs being unable to support the body."

Loon. Judith Hotchkiss, Deer Isle, Maine. 17" × 8". Oxford regular #10, 3-ply wool rug yarn.

"This loon was my first three-dimensional stuffed piece, and I completed it on a lake in northern Maine, listening to the real loons calling out on the water. Heaven! The learning was in the assembly, and I realized a gusset in the base would help it sit up on its own much better."

Swan. Judith Hotchkiss, Deer Isle, Maine. 24" × 20". Oxford regular #10, 3-ply wool rug yarn.

"The swan was punched with a very subtly overdyed natural yarn, which was a joy to punch with. The direction of hooking helped define the details of this all-white bird. Finishing the swan was more challenging than the other birds due to the size and the long, skinny neck, which had to be overstuffed in order to support itself and stay upright."

Wood Duck. Judith Hotchkiss, Deer Isle, Maine. 16" × 10". Oxford regular #10, 3-ply wool rug yarn.

"The coloring of the wood duck is spectacular, and it was so fun to punch this little bird."

Canada Goose. Judith Hotchkiss, Deer Isle, Maine. 20" × 11". Oxford regular #10, 3-ply wool rug yarn.

Judith Hotchkiss

Swan, loon, and mallard

Left to right: Loon, mallard, and wood duck
Mallard. Judith Hotchkiss, Deer Isle, Maine. 17" × 8".

"The male mallard is one of the most recognizable birds due to their distinct coloring. They are beautiful to look at and fun to punch."

INSTRUCTIONS FOR FINISHING DECOYS

by Judith Hotchkiss

Step 1: After punching the birds, it is a simple process to finish them. Press with a steam iron front and back. Cut out the punched design, leaving approximately 2" all the way around. Turn under, clipping where necessary, and steam again. Sew down as a hem. In tight areas or inside corners, it may be necessary to clip closely so that the hem will turn under neatly, so reinforce those close areas with glue or Fray Check to make sure the backing does not unravel. After hemming, steam the finished piece well.

Step 2: Next, trace the finished shape onto wool fabric for a back. Leave an extra ½" or so all the way around. Turn ½" edge under all the way around and steam. Sew the back and punched pieces together by hand from the right side, leaving approximately 4"–5" open on the bottom. Cut out another piece of wool in a simple oval shape as a gusset to fit into the bottom. This step will allow the stuffed piece to sit upright. Sew gusset into bottom opening, leaving an opening to allow stuffing.

Step 3: Stuff with poly fiberfill and leftover snippets. Add lavender if you like. Adding some weights such as aquarium gravel will give the finished bird added stability. Close remaining opening.

INSTRUCTIONS FOR FINISHING DUMMY BOARD:

To finish the bird as a freestanding dummy board, complete step 1 as above. Then trace the finished piece onto a piece of thin plywood. Paint the plywood a neutral color. After the paint is thoroughly dry, attach the punched piece to the plywood. If you want to be able to remove the piece from the wood at some point, attach using Velcro. Glue is a more permanent adhesive and may be used.

9
The Coral Project

Project design by Cotey Gallagher

AMY'S CORAL MAT

I asked artist Cotey Gallagher to design a project that could incorporate all of the techniques taught in this book: novelty yarns, yarn combinations, different punch needle sizes, sculpting, shading, fabric strips, and bead stitch. My only request was a wave border because I always wanted to punch waves with fingered shading and mock shading. Cotey drew graceful stylized waves and chose branch coral for the center. She added seaweed, sea flowers, and circles. The circles are open to interpretation. Are they stones? Sand dollars? I opted for bubbles.

I did not use every technique in this book. I did use shading (waves and seaweed), sculpting (coral), different punch needle sizes (Oxford fine #8, #9, #10, #13, and #14 and Oxford regular #10), and novelty yarns and yarn combinations (outlines of bubbles). All of the yarn was worsted-weight wool with the exception of the novelty yarn surrounding the bubbles and rug yarn for the border and whipping.

For my waves, the lighter whitecaps use fingered shading transitioning from medium to light with 4 values. The darker churning waves are mock shaded with 8 values including the 5 lightest values of Judith Hotchkiss Designs and Dyeworks Island Blue and 3 darker values from my stash including a blue-green variegated. I love throwing a variegated in with solids to shake things up and give a more interesting look. I used Oxford fine #14 for the whitecaps with one exception: the very top of the whitecap is a single row of white punched a tad higher with the Oxford fine #13 to simulate the froth at the top of a whitecap.

For the coral I used sculpting and shading. Each coral was punched with three values of Judith Hotchkiss Coral. I outlined with dark and filled in with two lights to accentuate the difference in loop heights. First, I outlined the coral with an Oxford fine #13. I punched one row inside that with an Oxford fine #10. The row inside that was punched with an Oxford fine #9 and there was room for a tiny bit of Oxford fine #8 inside that. Each loop was clipped before I did the next row and the overall shape was rounded off with bent-handled scissors to create a 3-dimensional look. Making the Sweater Letter Project was excellent training for this and I followed all the steps taught by Louise!

I mock shaded the seaweed with an Oxford fine #14 and 4 values of green. The sea flowers were punched with an Oxford fine #14 and yarn from my stash. I filled the bubbles with Judith Hotchkiss Island Blue outlined with one row of two separate fun shiny novelty yarn. The blue novelty was very thin so I doubled it but the coral and blue twist was the right weight to use alone. These fancy yarns came out a bit taller than the worsted-weight wool because they were slippery. I liked the effect since bubbles do rise to the top!

For my sandy background I used a lighter color in the middle and a subtly darker one outside the seaweed. Violet Jane Caribbean Sands worked well for the light and Violet Jane Desert Sands for the dark. These Violet Jane yarns were 3-ply rug yarn and I separated them, using a single ply in The Oxford fine #14. I love the slightly crinkly effect the separated plies created.

For the border I used two rows of wool rug yarn in an Oxford #10 regular with the stem stitch to give a crisp and uniform edge. Cotey Gallagher then whipped the piece with matching rug yarn.

This tropical project was a wonderful escape when I punched it in February during a month of Vermont snowstorms. Sometimes yarn colors really do have appropriate names: Island blue, Coral, Desert Sands, and Caribbean Sands were just what I needed. What will you do with your Coral Project? So many possibilities . . . the choice is yours!

Coral Mat. Designed by Cotey Gallagher. Adapted, color planned, and punched by Amy Oxford. 17" × 17". Wool and synthetic yarns on cotton monk's cloth.

Waves: Mock shading with worsted-weight yarn and Oxford fine #14. **Whitecaps:** Worsted-weight yarn with Oxford fine #13 and #14. **Sand:** Single strand from 3-ply rug yarn with Oxford fine #14. **Coral:** Shading (three values each) and sculpting with worsted-weight yarn and Oxford fine #8, #9, #10, and #13. **Seaweed:** Worsted-weight yarn with Oxford fine #14. **Flowers:** Worsted-weight yarn with Oxford fine #14. **Bubbles:** Worsted-weight yarn and novelty yarn with Oxford fine #14. **Border:** Rug-weight yarn with Oxford regular #10. **Whipping:** Rug-weight yarn.

LOUISE'S CORAL MAT

I love everything about Cotey Gallagher's beautiful *Coral* pattern. First of all, it's a wonderful example of an overall design concept that is perfectly suited to its subject matter. Both literally and figuratively, the broad border of undulating waves serves to contain the treasures of the deep blue sea. The pattern also is highly adaptable to a variety of fibers and punch needle techniques, and it makes a versatile textile to display in your home—because there is no up/down right/left, it can be used almost anywhere as floor, table top, or wall décor.

I color planned my version of *Coral* from the outside in, starting with those gorgeous waves. I chose three mildly variegated colors of Violet Jane rug yarn: Mid-Atlantic, Atlantic, and Atlantic Coast. I used bead stitch to transition from one blue to the next to emphasize movement and create even more color variation. When you consider that a two-color bead stitch row creates a third color—squint and you'll see!—it's a great technique to use when you want the effect of many subtle color variations, just like we see in nature. The whitecaps were punched with a novelty yarn combination and adds a texture that suggests frothiness. The combo includes mohair, chenille, slubby cotton, and gold metallic thread.

For the background I chose another Violet Jane rug yarn. This one is Caribbean Sand, a calming neutral that lets the rich reds, blue-greens, golds, magenta, and purple take center stage.

The three coral branches use six values of a rich red-orange. Multiple needle heights create the knobs, and I skipped heights in order to exaggerate the dimension (Craftsman settings 10, 8, and 6). I punched the longest contours of seaweed with blue-green dip-dyed yarn from my stash and the flowers with graduated petal lengths (ocean daisies!) in worsted-weight yarn. The flowers were worked in concentric circles from the inside to the outside, one circle each with Oxford fine point punch needle sizes 10, 9, and 8.

I intended to punch the stones and pebbles in shades of taupe using the sculpting technique, but as my own *Coral* story developed I knew I had to turn them into gold coins—buried treasure! I simply used a circle template to redraw the shapes. Cotey's expert use of negative space made it easy to put in my own detail while maintaining the integrity of her original design.

By the end of the project I was so enamored of that big border of waves that I couldn't bring myself to square off my mat. Instead I left it wavy, and ready for a tidy whipped edge.

Coral Mat. Designed by Cotey Gallagher. Adapted, color planned, and punched by Louise Kulp. 17" x 17". Wool and cotton yarns and metallic thread on cotton monk's cloth.
Waves: Shading and bead stitch with rug-weight yarn and Oxford regular #10. **Whitecaps:** Novelty yarn combination with Oxford regular #10. **Sand:** Rug-weight yarn with Oxford regular #10. **Coral:** Shading (six values) with rug-weight yarn and Craftsman's Punch Needle settings 6, 8, and 10. **Seaweed:** Rug-weight yarn with Oxford regular #10. **Flowers:** Worsted-weight yarn with Oxford fine #8, 9, and 10. **Gold coins:** Rug-weight yarn with Oxford regular #9 and 10.

Coral Project Pattern, Working Version. 16" × 16". Designed by Cotey Gallagher.

The pattern is available as a download at www.schiffercraft.com/intermediate&advancedpunchneedle.

10

Pieces to Learn From: Oxford Teacher Certification Rugs

by Amy Oxford

One of the requirements for Oxford Certification is to design a rug that is at least 2' × 3' and includes at least three of the six techniques taught in certification class. These are the same techniques included in this book: punching with novelty yarns and yarn combinations, using different Craftsman and Oxford Punch Needle sizes, sculpting, shading, punching with fabric strips, and the bead stitch. Some students pick three techniques, while others use all six techniques and every possible Oxford Punch Needle size and Craftsman's Punch Needle setting. Several have even made up their own techniques! For many certification students, this is the first time they've designed a rug, and is also the largest piece they have ever punched.

Oxford Certified Instructors share several qualities. They are professionally trained student-oriented teachers and experienced rug makers who offer advice and guidance for all skill levels. They are equally committed to tradition and innovation. Trusted members of the punch needle rug hooking community, they are committed to sharing the pleasure of creating, encouraging student development, exploring student potential, promoting high-quality craftsmanship, developing the craft of rug hooking, and promoting kindness and connection. Instructors love what they do and take having fun very seriously!

Take your time at cleaning up. It is the time to be thankful to your rug for looking so nice. It really deserves the cleaning up; touch it smoothly and arrange the loop-overs kindly. Do not be angry at the loop-overs; think of them as tricky loops and smile to them. —*Oxford Certified Instructor Agnes Durda, Miskolc, Hungary*

Feel at Home in the Arms of Woods. Oxford Certified Instructor Agnes Durda, Miskolc, Borsod-Abauj-Zemplen varmegye, Hungary. 40" × 28". **Columns:** Oxford fine #14 with 3-cut strips of wool fabric. Oxford regular #10 with 6-cut and 7-cut strips of wool fabric. **Windows and door frames:** Oxford fine #8 and #14 and Oxford regular #10 with worsted-weight wool yarn; **trees:** clipping and sculpting with Oxford regular #8 and rug-weight wool yarn; **sky and walls:** Oxford fine #14 and Oxford regular #10 with rug-weight and worsted-weight wool yarn; **black-and-white border:** Oxford fine #14 and worsted-weight wool yarn; **ball on top of column:** novelty yarn and sculpting with Oxford fine #8, #9, #10, #13, and #14 (all of the Oxford fine punch needle sizes).

"The art of Austrian visual artist and architect Friedensreich Hundertwasser inspired me. Working with punch needle really helps our hands and mind feel free, and I wanted to express that in my rug. This inspired me to create a rug where the mixture of the pattern and the materials reflect the feeling of nature."

PIECES TO LEARN FROM: OXFORD TEACHER CERTIFICATION RUGS

A Woman on a Speeding Horse Won't See It. Oxford Certified Instructor Christie Beniston. 36" × 24". **Crinoline in the skirt and chimney bricks:** Oxford regular #10 with wool fabric strips; **horse and rider:** Oxford regular #8 and rug-weight wool yarn; **veins in leaves:** Oxford fine #10 and rug-weight yarn; **apple:** sculpted with Oxford regular #8, #9, and #10 and the Craftsman's Punch Needle; **horse mane and tail:** Oxford #9 regular and novelty yarn; **horse:** Oxford regular #8 with multiple strands of wool yarn.

"This rug tells the story of my week of training to become an Oxford Certified Instructor and incorporates many of my observations from my week in Vermont, including the farmhouse, an apple from the orchard, and the chipmunk I thought was a rat. And that's me, on a borrowed Morgan horse, galloping into my career of teaching." [A note from Amy: "A woman on a speeding horse won't see it" is a saying we use at the Oxford Rug Hooking School when a mistake is so small no one will notice!]

September Sunflowers. Oxford Certified Instructor Heidi J. Martin, Melbourne, Florida. 36" × 24". **Seed head:** sculpting with Craftsman settings 1 through 10 and 2-ply wool rug yarn; **seed head center:** Oxford fine #13 with 2-ply and 4-ply wool rug yarn combined with metallic floss; **flower petals and leaves:** shading with Oxford regular #9 and 4-ply wool rug yarn; **background:** Oxford regular #9 and spot-dyed wool rug yarn.

"A project using multiple techniques, mixed fibers, and different punch needle sizes to showcase the complexity and versatility of this art. It exhibits sculpting, with concave and convex seed heads, metallic fibers, graded shading, and a spot dyed background showing movement in the sky."

Tree of Life. Oxford Certified Instructor Katie Stackhouse, Calgary, Alberta, Canada. 24" × 36". **Center stem and outer area of heart:** Oxford regular #9 with 8-cut wool strips; **center of heart and center top tulip:** mohair novelty yarn with Oxford regular #9; **background:** Oxford regular #10 with wool rug-weight yarn; **foreground:** Oxford regular #9 with wool rug-weight yarn; **birds, floral elements, leaves, remaining part of heart, and top tulip:** heirloom Romney worsted-weight yarn, using multiple strands.

"This piece was inspired by my German Canadian Mennonite heritage. In making it, I felt connected to my family and to generations past. I used multiple techniques, punch needle sizes, and fibers, which makes it a true testament to the versatility of the Oxford Punch Needle."

Brushstrokes. Advanced Oxford Certified Instructor Micah Clasper-Torch, Los Angeles, California. 24" × 36". **Yellow paint:** sculpting with Craftsman and Oxford regular #10; **white and pink paint:** Oxford fine #8 and worsted-weight wool yarn and Oxford regular #10 with rug-weight wool yarn; **turquoise paint:** shading with Craftsman settings 5–10.

"This piece was a true study in 'painting with wool'! I attempted to re-create the look of a small acrylic painting I made, from the blending colors, to the dripping paint, and even the thickness of the paint. To do this, I utilized three advanced techniques: mixing fine and regular needles, sculpting with the Craftsman needle, and shading."

230   PIECES TO LEARN FROM: OXFORD TEACHER CERTIFICATION RUGS

Choose Joy. Oxford Certified Instructor Rebecca Martin, Longmont, Colorado. 24" × 36". Overall technique uses multiple punch needles, and the loop height gets smaller as you go up the rug: Craftsman's Punch Needle and Oxford regular #8 for cattails, Oxford regular #9 for the water, Oxford regular #10 for the mountains, and Oxford fine #14 for the sky. **Border:** Oxford regular #10 with 7-cut wool fabric strips, Oxford regular #10 and hand-dyed rug yarn for the shading, and Oxford regular #8 for the leaves; **sky:** shading with Oxford fine #14 and hand-dyed worsted-weight rug yarn; **treeline:** novelty yarns with Oxford regular #9 using a variety of yarn weights, including bulky and doubled worsted weight.

"Punch needle rug hooking has brought so much joy into my life. This rug depicts the twin mountain peaks that rise above our town. I knew I wanted to create a piece that represented my home for my Oxford Certification Rug. I see the mountains as I drive around town, and I see my rug every day in my home. Both always remind me to choose joy in my life."

Left: *Unlimited Boundaries.* Oxford Certified Instructor Ingrid Hieronimus, Petersburg, Ontario, Canada. 40" × 26".

"I designed this piece because of my love of geometrics. All the scrolls and knots were traditionally hooked with wool flannel dip-dyed fabric. The rest of the rug was punched with an Oxford fine #11 and bits of sari ribbon to add a spark."

Waiting. Oxford Certified Instructor Hildegard Edling, Tivoli, New York. 36" × 24". A combination of traditional hooking with a rug hook and wool fabric strips and punch needle hooking with yarn. Traditional rug hooking: **ladies' hair:** 6-cut; **faces:** 4-cut; **eyeglasses**: 3-cut; **clothes:** 7-cut; **bench legs:** 7-cut. Punch needle rug hooking: **sky and grass:** Oxford regular #9 and rug-weight yarn; **bench:** Oxford regular #9 with novelty yarn.

"I always wanted to punch three women on a bench—I don't know why! What are they waiting for? I'll leave that up to the viewer."

If you're interested in becoming an Oxford Certified Instructor, teacher certification programs are offered by Advanced Oxford Certified Instructors both in person and online. Oxford Certified Instructors can receive ongoing support and educational opportunities through our nonprofit guild, The Oxford Punch Needle Instructors Guild (OPNIG).

For more information about teacher certification or to find an Oxford Certified Instructor, visit www.amyoxford.com.

OXFORD CERTIFIED INSTRUCTORS FEATURED IN THIS BOOK

Kris Andrews | Vermont | USA

Christie Beniston | California | USA

Cilla Cameron | Nottingham | England

Micah Clasper-Torch* | California | USA |

Agnes Durda | Miskolc | Hungary

Hildegard Edling | New York | USA

Colleen Faulkner | Missouri | USA

Cotey Gallagher* | Vermont | USA

Carol Gaylor | Ontario | Canada

Laurel Golden | Washington | USA

Ingrid Hieronimus | Ontario | Canada

Judith Hotchkiss* | Maine | USA

Yvonne Iten-Scott | Ontario | Canada

Louise Kulp* | Pennsylvania | USA

Kevin LeMoine* | New Brunswick | Canada

Heidi Martin | Florida | USA

Rebecca Martin | Colorado | USA

Margaret Mitchell | Ontario | Canada

Michelle O Driscoll* | Cork | Ireland

Alaina Roberts | Vermont | USA

Katie Stackhouse | Alberta | Canada

Kim Scanlan* | Minnesota | USA

Simone Vojvodin* | Ontario | Canada

Una Walker* | Oregon | USA

Heidi Whipple* | Vermont | USA

Kelly Wright* | Bavaria | Germany

*Advanced Oxford Certified Instructors (certified to teach others to be Oxford Certified Instructors)

Index

Andrews, Kris, 67, 94

beading stitch
  basics, 171
  border, 166–167, 169, 170
  combining needle sizes, 53
  counting holes, 172
  envy, 174
  on the curve, 170
  showing, 51
  tips, 172
  two-color, 51, 53–54, 56–57, 162–174, 216, 218–219, 224

Beniston, Christie, 175, 226, 234

border
  beading stitch, 166–167, 169, 170
  counting holes, 172
  crocheted, 156
  drawing, 78
  mitered corner, 167
  proddy, 159
  scroll, 75
  steam pressing, 23, 88
  wave, 216, 218

Briggs & Little, 159

budget, 18, 43–44

Cameron, Cilla, 125, 132, 157, 234
Campbell, Patricia B., 100, 107
carrier, 30
Certification rugs, 224–233
Chéticamp, 135–136
Clasper-Torch, Micah, 48, 222, 229, 234
coasters, 18, 44, 94
coloring in pattern, 50–51
Coral Project, 216–220
cordoning off, 32
corners, mitered, 167
course correction, 86
Craftsman's Punch Needle (the Craftsman), 12, 28, 42–44, 47, 49, 51, 53–55, 76, 90, 94–95, 141, 219, 224, 226–227, 229, 231

cutters
  fabric, 139
  rotary, 135

decoys, finishing, 213
designs, elements of, 166
directional punching, 31, 90, 104, 110, 115, 150
documenting your artwork, 33
doodle cloths, 26–28, 30, 32–33
dummy board, finishing, 213
Durda, Agnes, 225, 234
dyeing, 108, 182, 185
  formulas, 105, 108, 167–168, 185
  Primary Fusion, 108
  PRO Chemical, 108, 185

edges
  beveled, 86
  mitered, 150, 167, 170, 172
  whipped (also called whip stitching), 58, 92, 216–218

Edling, Hildegard, 233, 234
Emilio 20, font, 78
emphasizing points, 118

Faulkner, Colleen, 11, 180–195, 234
Field, Jeanne, 104
finishing methods, 23, 32, 88, 151, 210–211, 213
fleece, polar, 161
Flower Project, introduced, 134–135
Fluff & Peachy Bean Designs, 142
frames
  and novelty yarn, 28
  gripper strip, 26, 28, 33, 85
free-form, 76, 96

Gallagher, Cotey, 12, 48, 64, 76–77, 130, 164–165, 177–179, 214, 216–220, 234
garments, 44
Gaylor, Carol, 98, 176, 234
Golden, Laurel, 160, 234
Green, Jane Halliwell, 104
Gripper strips, 69, 71–73, 78–79, 82–83
Gunarta, Adien, 78

Hannum, Peggy, 112, 119
Harrison, Ted, 198
Harrisville Designs, 42, 61

Hearts Sampler Project, introduced, 41
  Simplified version, 60–63
hemming, 32–33, 59, 213
herringbone, 140
Hieronimus, Ingrid, 99, 108, 166, 232, 234
hook, crochet, 151–156
Hotchkiss, Judith, 124, 210–213, 234

In a Nutshell (chapter summary), 18, 43, 75, 104, 135, 167
International Guild of Handhooking Rugmakers, The (TIGHR), 198
Iten-Scott, Yvonne, 34, 158, 234

Judith Hotchkiss Designs and Dyeworks, 103, 131, 151, 168, 216

layers, punching in, 189–191
Lemoine, Kevin, 159, 161, 234
line
  curved, 138. With beading stitch, 170; with fabric strips, 138
  dotted, 57, 166, 168
  grid, 120, 202
  holding, 146–147, 149
  police, 32
  Sharpie, 31, 131
  straight, 158
loop
  align before cutting, 74
  alternating, 167
  clipped (cut open), 78–79, 83–85, 92–93, 95, 97, 119, 216, 224
  fabric strip, twisted, 138
  height, 12, 43, 44, 47, 53, 58, 79, 90, 92, 140–141, 216, 231
  intermingling, 83
  loop-overs, 224
  pulling, 92, 104
  sculpting, 73
  sewing on beads, 128

magazine, *Rug Hooking*, 4, 108
Maine, Broad Bay, 75, 78, 86
maintaining shape, 31
Martin, Heidi J., 128, 129, 227, 234

Ontario Hooking Craft Guild (OHCG), 198
ornaments, 44
overpacking (jam-packed), 27, 57, 92, 113–114, 158
Oxford Certified Instructors and Advanced Oxford Certified Instructors, about, 13, 224, 233–234
 Certification projects, 224–233
Oxford Punch Needle
 choosing, 43–44
 combining multiple sizes, 42, 49, 75, 53, 218, 224, 231
 combining with the Craftsman's Punch Needle, 49, 76–77
 complete sets, 45, 53
 fine point, 47
 guarantee, 29
 inventor, 239
 lifetime
 matching size with strip width, 139
 mini, 48
 mini with heels, 48
 regular point, 47
 screw eyes, 17, 29
 sizes, 39–70, 75, 79, 138, 217–218, 224; explanation of, 45–47
 stitch gauge, 21, 27, 92
 with fabric strips, 139, 158, 161, 224
 with multiple strands of yarn, 18–21, 24–25, 29, 31, 33, 37
 with novelty yarn, 18–29
 with polar fleece, 161
Oxford Punch Needle Instructors Guild (OPNIG), 233
Oxford Rug Hooking School, 6, 8, 226, 239

padula, 69
pen, Mark-B-Gone / water-soluble, 103, 114, 117
Perfectly Paisley Project, introduced, 164–166
plaid, 51, 53–54, 56–59, 61, 63
planning of projects, 51
polar fleece, punching with, 161
Primary Fusion, 108
primitive, 105, 109, 138
projects: Coral, 216; Flower, 134; Hearts Sampler, 41; Perfectly Paisley, 164; Seashell, 16; Shaded Leaves, 102; Simplified Hearts Sampler, 60; Sweater Letter, 72
PRO Chemical dyes, 108, 185

Martin, Rebecca, 69, 230–231, 234
Maw & Co., 122
McAdoo Rugs, 12
McGown, Pearl, 69, 104, 106
Merrett, Patricia, 182
mirror imaging, 50, 144, 145
Mitchell, Margaret, 196–209, 234
Moshimer, Joan, 104
multistranding, 187, 189
multivalue shading. See *shading*
nail brush, 74, 87

natural fibers, defined, 19
needle
 Clover-brand jumbo tapestry, 74, 83, 179
 knitting, 4, 58–59, 63, 74, 83, 87, 93, 150
 punch. See *punch needle*
Nokomis, 198

O Driscoll, Michelle, 36, 68, 234
Olson, Jane, 104

pro tips, 29, 34, 49, 52, 53, 57, 58, 83, 85, 86, 95, 113, 118, 120, 146, 187, 189, 191
punch needle
    choosing, 43
    Craftsman, The. See *Craftsman's Punch Needle*
    Oxford, The. See *Oxford Punch Needle*
Puzzle of Love (Louise Kulp), as project basis, 40–59

reverse punching, 69
Roberts, Alaina Dickason, 131, 234
row spacing, 21, 27, 50, 92, 113, 184
rug hook, traditional (tool), 151, 233
Rug Hooking magazine, 4, 108

samplers, 49
Scanlan, Kim, 14, 35, 64, 126, 159, 234
scissors, bent-handled, 58, 74, 86, 90, 93, 103, 119, 216
screw eyes, 17–18, 29
scrubby, 74, 87–88, 135, 151
sculpting, 64, 70–100, 205, 216–218, 224, 226–227, 229
Seal Harbor Rug Company, 103, 168
Seashell Project, introduced, 16–17
Shaded Leaves Project, introduced, 102–103
shading, 104–129, 182–195
    diagrams, 110–111, 116–117
    eight-value, 172
    Faulkner, Colleen, 184–187
    fine, 9, 66, 97, 105, 127, 130
    fingering technique, 102–103, 107, 109, 110, 115–122, 125, 129–130, 184, 216
    mock technique, 76, 103, 107, 109, 110, 112, 114, 116, 121–122, 129, 177, 216–217
    multivalue, 104, 166
    pencil-shaded drawings, 110–113, 116
    resources, 104
    value-on-value, 129
    with yarn, 11, 180–195
Shaped Butterfly Mat, 89–92
Shepherd, Gene, 104
Simplified Hearts Sampler Project, introduced, 60–63
special effects
    multivalue combinations, 31
    plaid, 56
    stripes, 30–31

tweeds, 30
Stackhouse, Katie, 65, 228, 234
steam pressing, 18–19, 23, 32–33, 49, 58–59, 88, 92, 128, 150–151, 213
stitches
    gauge, 21, 27, 92
    jumping over, 63, 177
    size, 21, 27, 50, 92, 113, 217, 184
    stem stitch, 37, 96, 177, 179, 216
storytelling, in rug design, 198–209
strand-along, 30
stranding, 49
stripes, 30, 53–54, 56, 168
strips, fabric, 135–161
    combining with yarn, 233
    cutter, 135, 138–139
    preparing wool, 141
    punching, 183–185
    reducing waste, 152–153
    weight, 140, 161
    wide-cut, 105
    width and punch needle sizes, 138–139
    wool, choosing, 140
    wool, synthetic or blend, 19
suppliers, yarn and wool
    Briggs & Little, 159
    Fluff & Peachy Bean Designs, 142
    Harrisville Designs, 42, 61
    Judith Hotchkiss Designs and Dyeworks, 103, 131, 151, 168, 216
    Seal Harbor Rug Company, 103, 168
    Violet Jane Rug Yarn, 8, 74, 103, 168, 216, 218, 239
    Whackadoo Yarns, 184
swatches, 104–105, 142
sweater depiller, 33, 59, 88, 103, 119, 151, 172
Sweater Letter Project, introduced, 72–73
synthetic fibers, defined, 19

threader, 43
threads
    as fibers for punching, 18–19, 22, 24, 33
    defined, 19
3D approaches, 75, 78, 97, 159, 192, 210–213, 216
topographic
    effect, 67
    map of project, 79–80

traditional rug hooking, 9, 104–105, 108, 111, 119, 135, 138, 140–141, 151, 166, 174
troubleshooting, 28, 30
tweed, 30, 140
tweezers, 74, 86
twill, 140

Violet Jane Rug Yarn, 8, 74, 103, 168, 216, 218, 239
Vojvodin, Simone, 70, 97, 98, 99, 234

Waldoboro, 75, 78, 86
Walker, Una, 37, 96, 156, 234
Whackadoo Yarns, 184
Whipple, Heidi, 35, 125, 133, 157, 234
wool fabric
    choosing 140
    herringbone, 140
    strips, 132–161
    synthetic or blend, 19
    tweed, 140
    twills, 140
Wright, Kelly, 66, 95, 127, 155, 234

yarn
    acrylic, 17, 19, 20
    cashmere, 22
    characteristics, 24
    choosing, 19–20, 23, 28, 49, 51
    color cards, 108
    combinations, 17–37, 47, 216, 218, 224
    knitting, 20, 22
    multivalue combinations, creating, 20, 31
    natural fibers, 19, 23
    novelty, 14–37, 44, 47, 216, 224
    polyester, 17, 19, 23
    preparing combinations, 24
    silk, 19, 22, 25, 28–29
    synthetic fibers, 19, 23, 32
    texture, 19, 22, 24–25, 30, 136, 161, 166, 172, 218
    thickness, 21, 24–25, 43, 109
    weights, 20–21, 24–25, 47, 49, 90, 92
yarn and wool fabric suppliers. See *suppliers, yarn and wool*

About the Authors

Photo: Sam Interrante

LOUISE KULP

Louise Kulp was academically trained as a painter, fiber artist, and art educator. In 2006 she learned punch needle rug hooking from Amy Oxford, and it quickly became her medium of choice for creative expression and teaching. In 2018 she earned certification as an Advanced Oxford Certified Instructor, with a focus on special techniques.

Louise has taught the joy of punch needle rug hooking to hundreds of students in many different settings, from women in a grief support group in rural Maine to second graders in an after-school program in the Bronx, New York.

Her background in painting informs her current studio work in rug hooking: she draws still lifes directly onto stretched monk's cloth with charcoal and then applies color, using hand-dyed wool. And she still loves technique *almost* as much as she loves making pictures.

Louise lives and works in Lancaster County, Pennsylvania.

AMY OXFORD

Amy Oxford is the inventor of the Oxford Punch Needle, a tool that has become the gold standard in the punch needle world. Punch needles have been around since 1881, but Amy's goal was to create an ergonomic tool that would reduce repetitive-motion injuries. The tools are easy to use and have become trusted friends to fiber artists around the world.

Amy learned to make punch needle–style hooked rugs in 1982, when she discovered her dream job working as a rug puncher for McAdoo Rugs, a cottage industry in North Bennington, Vermont. An internationally renowned instructor, Oxford has loved teaching the craft since 1986. She has been licensed by the Shelburne Museum to make adaptations of their antique rugs and has helped catalog the museum's collection of over 400 hooked rugs. She is the past president of the Vermont Crafts Council and past vice president of the Green Mountain Rug Hooking Guild.

Amy is the author of six books, including *Punch Needle Rug Hooking: A Complete Resource to Learn & Love the Craft*. Her work has been exhibited throughout New England and in the United Kingdom.

Amy is the founder of The Oxford Rug Hooking School, in Cornwall, Vermont. The school offers classes and retreats for all skill levels, including teacher certification. Amy also owns Violet Jane, a yarn-dyeing business specializing in hand-painted variegated rug yarns that are dyed at the school.

www.amyoxford.com

"If you are truly excited about what you are making, others will see it, and the best part? You will feel it!"

—Amy Oxford